鷹巢

AERIE

Up On Big Rock Poetry Series
SHIPWRECKT BOOKS PUBLISHING COMPANY
Winona, Minnesota

鷹巢

AERIE

DAN BUTTERFASS

Cover and interior design by Shipwreckt Books
Cover painting, *Good Morning America,* by Steve Delaitsch

Shipwreckt Books Publishing Company
357 W. Wabasha Street
Winona, Minnesota 55971

Library of Congress Control Number: 2024932525

I rode back through the woods of Turgenev's Spasskoye in the evening light: fresh greenery in the woods and under foot, stars in the sky, the scent of flowering willow, and wilting birch leaves, the sound of the nightingale, the hum of beetles, the cuckoo and solitude, and the pleasant, vigorous movement of the horse under you, and health of body and mind. And I thought, as I constantly think, of death.
§ *Tolstoy, in a letter to his wife*

Every instant of our lives is essentially irreplaceable: you must know this in order to concentrate on life.
§ *Andre Gide*

Every creative act is an act of hypocrisy and violence. You may have to think about it for a while, but I am sure you can discover your own.
§ *Mary Ruefle*

It was love, the furnace into which everything was dropped. Summer mornings, the light of the world pouring in and the silence. It was a barefoot life, the cool of the night on the floorboards, the green trees if you stepped outside, the first faint cries of the birds.
§ *James Salter*

Contents

Art and Life

At the city compost site
Ringed by chain link

Spring wind rushes
Into a mountain

Of discarded Christmas
Trees unearthing moist

Currents of scent
Stronger than portaging

All one distant
Summer of Duluth

Packs strapped
Front & back

Through boreal
Forest infinite

With spruce and fir
Cedar and pine

Holy Grail of Carp

The grail is being in perfect accord with Nature's abundance.
—Joseph Campbell

I forgot to tell you about the unalloyed
joy of spearing carp making their spring
spawning runs up shallow clear creeks
flowing under country bridges all across
the Midwest, out to which we boys rode
our bikes with primitive spears balanced
deftly across the handlebars, eager to test
our skills against quarry that glided
upstream at the speed of phantoms
the instant they sensed our ulterior
presence, the apprentice throws almost
always errant or too late as the
school shot forward into a culvert's
darkness, the surface already rippling
with the raw power of more
and more carp, foreign and unwanted
with pursed lips and gelatinous Fu
Manchu whiskers, denizens infesting a cattail
slough's marl, except in spring when they
ran up clear creeks to spawn and we
boys rode our bikes out to bridges
on a quest for the living heft—
to feel spear tines thrust just once
through the slimy keratinous armor,
razor points emerging from the saffron
belly-bulge, pierced and thrashing the gentle

current, then hoisted flopping in new
tufts of spring with flared gills and
big stunned convex eye brimming
revelry as we boys circle shouting as if
this dance will last the rest of our lives.

My Neighbor's Elm

Staring at my neighbor's great elm,
I remember my grandfather:
smell of gas on his hands
and thin moons of his fingernails
stained by the work he loved—
greasing a tractor, changing
oil on his Chrysler.
I can see him shuffling
in denim coveralls
down the frost-heaved sidewalk
on his way in for the noon meal,
sauerkraut and blood
sausage frying on the stovetop;
I hear the clack
of his false teeth as he chews,
and see the two trees in his yard—
one a plum that sent some
of its sweetness into the grass
each fall; and the other an elm
like my neighbor's
with its great upwelling
of branches, its heavy
fountain of leaves pooling
an oasis of shade on the lawn.
I remember the bare plot
after the tree was cut,
the unsettled mound
of sunlit black dirt.

I remember its great girth:
how two grown men,
my father and grandfather
reaching around the trunk,
could not join hands.

No One Ever Dies
for Ed Sharkey, 1919-1997

Dead these past ten years,
it's not for me to explain
how your soul finds a new
home in weathered barn boards,
in the woven ash of a tattered
paper wasp nest swaying empty
from winter's aspen branch; how
you sometimes inhabit the cedar
of half-sunken docks; you move
freely wherever I go, from one
gray transient thing to
another: driftwood we gathered
and lit on a cold August
beach as a squall blew in
off Superior; the ashes I scoop
from the hearth and spread
on your granddaughter's perennial
beds moist with March
snowmelt; a bleached Ojibwa
canoe paddle washed to shore
just after ice-out, crude and strong
as the year it was carved, so that
on hot afternoons at the cabin
I can dip the blade of your face
into glints of ascension
light rippling cool water.

Figure Skater: Winter 1976
for D.L

That tall, lithe girl who figure
skated each morning before
the school bell, whose solo
performances I never
missed—a mediocre
skater holding onto an excuse
of hockey stick, fumbling
a puck around her pirouettes
of spiraling grace; her blonde hair
rippling, she was a seabird
whirling on gusts of her own
twenty-knot wind, her aerial
leaps like a family of deer that
sometimes startled from a clearing
along the rink, and bounded
away through our hushed
stadium of winter oaks, colorless
as the black-and-white
screen on which I dream
we're young Olympians, gold
medalists edging by a tenth
of a point the favored Soviets
as an astonished crowd roars
in slow-motion to its feet,
the silent applause of millions
of snowflakes drifting thick
as confetti as our routine

ends and I wake still
dreaming her, my palms
sweaty, our hands almost
touching thirty years later.

Lilacs

slow amble down the sidewalk
through the oldest part of the city
into the fragrance of porch
garden and shedside
groves of lilac

cast iron yard pump
  picket fence
    carriage house
      old chicken coop

each with its drooping
sprigs of moist art
gentle emigrant perfume
of Grandmother's jar
of kitchen-table lilacs

an apparition within each grove
where faces lost since childhood
multiply in reverse of time, one
face then another rising
into the mind's riparian glow
as if woven and unwoven
by moving looms
of creek light

one face then another
momentarily clear
down through the merge
swirl and churn of silent currents

sometimes a face with a name
moving at slow creek speed
eddying out from where it was lost
in the eternal repose of my heart's shadow,
now made of water's
ceaseless flow, luminous
in the scent of lilacs

faces that no longer exist
lost early in childhood
as if far back in the light
of unremembered dreams,
or further back in the light
of memories passed down
from before birth,
or ones that return with death,
now rising to the surface as if from a long-ago
country that no longer exists, even
as it reveals faces of trudging old men
and wrinkled old women hanging laundry
and faces of schoolmates unworn
by time—

who no longer exist, even
as I carry them inside, except
in early May walking
through groves of lilac

Wrens

Just yesterday my grandmother
knelt in her garden

this morning staked
her tomatoes, only

an hour ago, pinned damp
sheets to the clothesline

under a blossoming plum,
where the wren that just flew

into its quarter-size hole
peers out nesting half

a lifetime later inside
the present moment

of this birdhouse my daughter
painted in primary colors.

After Reading Proust

I never could
bear to be inside
before, as right now,
with sunrise
like honey smeared
across the lawn,
in this room at my desk,
in May with bluebells
and anemone flooding
the loamy swales;
with the lilacs
in full bloom
along the garden shed
almost promising
that I might,
in today's sudden heat
after last night's
soaking rain, stumble
upon morels, just-
birthed
in new moss,
amid prickly ash,
under dead elms.

It's still agony
at times
not to walk out
from this interior
shade,
into the moist

art of wildflowers
and soft ricochet
of warblers
above a sweep
of river current;

though now, half
way downstream
from when I began
this life, the river
of my body
has molded itself
into an eddy
from which more
often than not
I'm content
to peer out
at the same scene
from the same room,
as strangely enamored
as those first
bees I saw
four times yesterday
in the boulevard
grass (twice
in the morning
walking my daughter
to school and twice
in the afternoon
walking her home)—

that with so many other
sources of nectar
to choose from
instead
spent all day
mining
down
through
a shaft
the sweet
inside the dark
of a discarded
soda can.

Spring Suite

This morning in Minneapolis
hungover and in need
of an earthen
music that restores
this moment-by-moment
world to its own magic
bird song
leaf flutter
ocean surf
of a not-distant freeway,
a low passenger jet's tornadic
roar amid the south wind's soft
hiss in shoreline reeds
at Lake of the Isles.
Nearing a canal marsh,
I hear the boom and croak
of my mind coming back to life.
§
Mired now and here
in songs of asphalt,
refrains of weedy
broken concrete,
leitmotif of dandelions
pushing their wildness up
through cracks in city sidewalk.
§
My *duende* hardened
from disuse, a lump
of torpor lodged in my soul:
On a Loring Park bench

I wait long
hours for it to pass
in agony
like a kidney stone.

§

Through cracked
stained glass the devout
chant, reciting a liturgy's
drone of petrified poetry,
as sap seeps from a gash
in the side of a sugar maple.

§

Maybe we only have as many
friends as we have selves
to give to, inventing
for each one an authentic
version of the same person?
Having "gone home" I decided
I should stop by to see an old
friend. He showed me his nice yard;
I said hello to his nice wife, met
his son and daughter, also very nice.
The two cars parked in his driveway
were nice. Even his dog, a border
collie, was nice. We shook hands
and he said it was nice to see me.

§

I know they are the tips of *hostas*
yet upon waking still need to ask
(as if in a single night
I could sleep my way back
into the body of the child

I once was) what rough
blind winter-tormented
beast gropes for sunlight
thrusting its pointed
claws up through the soil?
                    §
Suddenly the one who becomes
your soul mate catches
the invisible breeze drifting
out from your gaze, her aura
like leaves of a single
outlying aspen trembling
their first pastel blush
against the stillness of the rest
of a forest's near-infinite
mass of undifferentiated trees.
                    §
Weathered grey cedar worn smooth
by the scuffing of his work boots—
bleached by sun, battered
by rain, waves, ice, sleet, snow, hail—
the boards of a dock that once led
through water lilies out onto the lake
now hang from an alfalfa field's fence
posts three hundred miles from the cabin,
with bluebirds nesting against his footsteps.
                    §
Those peerless mornings
of light cold rain pattering
a backpacker's tent,
when you wake to the face
of the other who first

blinded you to time,
are peerless
because they only
happen once.
Except while asleep, dreaming
the body of the other
in absolute clarity,
the same moments
unfolding as if for the first
time ceaselessly flowing.

§

What is
the third eye,
the fifth dimension,
the sixth sense,
the seventh direction?

Day's infinite blue,
night's infinite black?
When you look up
at the sky, do you
ever ask yourself,
What is the stars,
what is the stars?

Explain the universe.
How did it all begin,
and how will it end?
O me! O life! What is
our purpose if any
under the sun, why
are we even here?

What of the stone
after it's thrown?
The word after
its spoken?
The occasion
after it's missed?
Time after its gone?

You can't even
define poetry,
she demanded
as we walked
a gravel road's
fence line
plum thickets
snowing blossoms
into the ditch,
a pheasant
strutting out
disappearing
into the brush.
§
In my dream she handed me
the eros of her love poem
scrawled on a rapid
succession of restaurant
napkins, every stanza
like flashes of heat
lightening, humid,
atmospheric as a first
spring thunderstorm. Still moist

just before I woke, her lines
clear as sunlight,
quickly evaporated.
Hiking a storm-dampened
forest, I strained to remember
words blown farther away
with each fresh gust of wind,
stray fragments of their music
dripping from the leaves.

§

Following a bosky deer trail
through the shallowest
muck of a cattail slough,
out to a knob-and-kettle island
of maples, once a sugarbush
where no roads or bridges lead,
I spot a stand of freshly dead
elms with the bark peeling off
in long, loose strips: *wolf
trees*, they're called, as if
the trunk's been raked
by canine claws. I can hear
my heart in my chest
beating like the onset of hard
spring rain. Wending
through prickly ash,
kneeling among sunlit
tufts of new moss,
almost as if
they were a blessing,
I find a patch of morels.
Then another flourish,

more in profusion across
the forest floor, a mother-
lode of serendipity
that will take hours
to harvest. I hold a first
up to my nose, so curiously
shaped like a man, inhaling
the scent of a woman.

§

In rich moist bottomland forest
unearthing as the Dakota once did
miniature chestnut-shaped roots
of Spring Beauty—their system
of runners impossibly lymphatic,
tubers hidden, difficult
to locate, small and hard
as the bean-sized nodes
in my groin and armpits.

§

Last night I dreamt
the moment I die I'll swim
naked among brook trout,
in a passage from a book
I read before
its author wrote it,
my next body *polished,*
muscular and torsional,
the white edges of my fins
wimpling softly in the amber
flow. On our backs
are vermiculate patterns,
maps and mazes

of the world
in its becoming, ones
I've held in my hands before
far *older than man,*
the mystery of their origin
luminous and humming
in early morning sunlight.

§

Wanting my mind, along with my life,
to mold itself in the image of a river,
I went canoeing down the Zumbro
an everyday not-so-famous tributary
of a larger river that like all rivers
(except for those possessed by dams)
flows in its ceaseless present moment
without once pausing to consider itself.

§

If only I could live at the speed
at which time actually moves,
I'd rush fast and clear as riffles,
more swiftly as rapids, the waves
of a run shaped by submerged
boulders; subside into a slow
deep calm dark pool, swirl
sidelong as a cutbank eddy
that circles back on itself,
rise as an upwelling bulge
from beneath a logjam,
sweep into a sharp bend,
plunge against rock face,
pillow softly over a boulder,
drift in slow meander,

keep flowing downstream
with the total acceptance
and humility of creek water.

§

Here I am, already in the second
of three (and trailing edge
of a fourth) generation the green
fuse of time keeps alive at every
given moment, among the newest
living outer rings of a primordial
near immortal family tree (its seedling
sprouted some 2.5 million years ago)
grown immense with heartwood,
dense with epochs of the dead
supporting a vast swaying canopy,
only these thin spherical layers—
xylem, cambrium, phloem—still
flowing with the living sap,
irrepressible and unbidden force
that through a thin green fuse
drives the tendril flower of buds
unfurling into new leaves.

§

This one life's an indefinite
reprieve—the birth of each
spring brings on an ache
of joy stronger than the last—
while the father who is son
to the man in me keeps on
wishing it would never end.

1994

Incantation for My Wife

Because sudden overnight flourishes
of dandelions have blatantly
overwhelmed whole green fields
with brilliant seams of gold

Because just now the moon rises
from silhouetted treetops
like a woman stepping out
from an evening dress

Because the sheen of your auburn
hair wavers like firelight
in the anterior of my ribcage

Because the water table suddenly
higher with new rain
presses up through the porous
seep of our basement floor

Because in the absolute dark
at the bottom of an ancient ocean's
bedrock upon which our house is built
the phosphorescence by which we'll dream
arrives unbidden and without source

Because the lead of a V of hard-
flying spring geese bound for the far
north with outstretched necks strains
for their destination with guttural
chants and a lissome whoosh
of overhead wing beats

Because the children are asleep

Mother's Milk

Robins tenderizing earthworms
hopped through the luxuriance
of wet sunny grass, worm parts dribbling
from sharp beaks as they chirped
praises for an abundance the night's soft
rain had lured up through the soil
to be regurgitated down blind hatchlings'
yammering throats. This almost
impossible morning for high-pitched
squeals of manic anguish from red
tulip beds, I whistled and happy music
jangled from Rose's tags as she trotted
over clutching tighter with a grinning
muzzle the live, now crushed plaything
for which there was nothing to be done
except order her to release the wailing
baby rabbit and end its suffering. No
doubt one of earth's several billion
sad mothers still awaits its safe return
under the garden shed. When I missed
its neck with a glistening spade, the full
stomach exploded onto bare shins, a hot
white splatter of pristine curds that Rose,
an innocent of the cosmos, licked
from my legs with an indifferent tongue,
though perhaps she dimly recalled suckling
Mom for whom she yelped and whimpered
shivering with a runt's fear and longing
for her siblings as I orphaned her away.

Young Tolstoy at his Writing Desk

Is it that there's only one, only one?
That from the beginning to the end
of life there should only be one
like one white pine that's taller than
all the rest along the ridge outside
your window? Only one who flares
inside you like the first pastel blush
of spring in the birch-trees; from
the first to the last dawn, only one
waiting in some distant station
with whom to exchange a single fatal
glance, an instant of recognition
that she will always be the only
one who you want beside you
at your deathbed? And if her
touch were lost, what then?
Would it surge through you
with the moon's unwavering
pull on an ocean, each memory
of her hands like an incoming
tide that sends tremors of longing
through the marrow of your body?
Or would the now invisible water
of her hands harden in your soul
like the pattern and swirls of grain
in this oak writing desk, the flow
that's receded and suspended within
all lustrous things made of wood?

Blind Ben's List

lilacs in bloom
along the sidewalk
  trash cans
when it's starting to get warm
  a cigarette on a very
cold morning, *Nag Champa*
  a little dark bar
when it's very hot, the stale
  beer and old smoke, a bakery
any time, airports because
  you are going somewhere,
street food frying, hippies'
  stench but only till
three days after bathing, bongo
  drumming, draft horse
barns at the fair, tropical forest
  dripping after rain, fresh
split firewood, temblors before
  a thunderstorm, belly
laughter, waking to wind
  chimes or a train
whistle in the night, cicadas,
  slow-moving water, rush hour
traffic at a distance, campfire
  crackling new wood, first
strums of a guitar, children
  on a playground, baseball
but only on the radio

§ *found in a notebook after my next-door neighbor died at thirty*

Memorial Day

A flag hangs limp
Uninspired from its pole

Steam rises straight up from the brick chimney
Of a hospital's power plant

Dissolving into blue sky
The way grief

Finally leaves the body

Because the budding tips of pines
Are holding out their new green

And every baby born to someone you know
That you have ever touched

Has extraordinarily perfect
Tiny feet and toes

Natural World

Each time our canoe drifts
around a new bend of river

closing in as we cast our lures,
the same great blue heron lifts

from its vigil on a logjam
gliding the tree-lined corridor,

out of sight as the river curves
concealing itself the moment

it reveals each future stretch
always disappearing

just beyond the next bend,
like a realm we'll never reach

no matter how far we float,
the current drawing us closer

as we drift back into view,
the heron indifferent, as if asleep,

then slowly exploding
with immense and labored

wingbeat to keep a precise
distance from the world of men.

Generose

Sparrows cutting their mouths on dawn
sing that the mad dwell across the street,
where from the pattern of lighted windows
silhouetted faces stare into the blue dark.
With full daylight, this shrill bleeding
grows less shrill and they're granted
walks through my neighborhood, stroll
the courtyard of the Peace Garden
pausing for benediction at the statue
of St. Francis, robed with a songbird
perched on his shoulder as he bends
to tame the marauding wolf of Gubbio.
The mad mill about in street clothes,
they mingle and sit reasonably
across from us on park benches
as my young daughter tosses pennies
into a rushing fountain—our own idle
form of madness. They join the crowd
of other patients, of orderlies and nurses
in their solid burgundy uniforms
who flock at each change of shift
to smoke on the corner along the row
of cone-laden evergreens that lies
as a buffer between my house and the Sister
Mary *Generose* building, where the mad
from far-flung places live for weeks
or months that may or may not
turn into numb years of posing
wordless questions into the blue dark
through their rooms' narrow, lighted windows.

If only we could see the nodes and motes
of madness in their eyes the way the winter-
bare deciduous trees reveal the balled,
leafy clumps of squirrels' nests now
hidden by summer foliage. If only one
of the mad would step out right now
from the *Generose* building and begin
preaching softly aloud to the roosting,
brawling sparrows—if only one of the mad
would show us how to talk to the animals,
calming the wary squirrels and rabbits
my daughter would like to touch and hold,
then all this shrill bleeding might be stopped
turning a single healing word *Generose*
over and over on the threshold of our tongues.

Wood Day

Every October during that
decade of heating
our house with diseased
elm, of carting and stacking
and handing split logs
through the glowing forge
of a basement window
after school at dusk,
his forehead dripping
the sweat of a life sentence
to what he called *this*
grim outpost, my father
would nudge me awake
early, with stern
glee on wood day,
hard labor I hated more
than the interminable
hour of the bony knuckles
of my young ass
strapped by tradition
to a church pew, the hydraulic
drone of the wood-
splitter and sour
fungoid odor of juice surging
from the stringy
elmwood as the blunt
wedge strained
into the tree's fat waist, often
getting stuck while
the machine bucked
and moaned its protest.

Lust in the Heart for Rose the Dog and Jimmy Carter

Don't wander the produce aisles
Jimmy, during Indian summer when you'll
be tempted to examine too many smooth
browned arms and legs during this last
week of sundresses, or linger
too long in the scent
suspended over bins
of McIntosh—and you might
try going to the grocery store
in sweaty blaze
orange and hunting boots trailing
mud across the fresh polish, your hands
and cheeks etched by blackberry
bramble. But Jimmy, I'm somehow
saved by glancing back at my
Lab girlfriend's sad
devoted eyes through the driver's
side window, and by the nagging
worry that someone might
pry the truck door open
or smash the glass and take her
away while my eye
wanders from leeks and ripe tomatoes
and lingers too long as I fill
my wife's list. Nevertheless,
Jimmy, I'm saved by Rose
as she watches me grow
smaller across the parking lot

and vanish through automatic
doors, as she waits with raised
and expectant eyelashes, a peculiar
tilt and crinkle to her forehead, worried
or certain, Jimmy, I'm never coming back.

Collision

The night he struck a deer
that totaled his car he came home
shaken by the jolt that whiplashed
his neck and sent a great doe hurtling
in slow-motion over the windshield,
already dead, as if beached
on the frozen median ditch.
He watched his hand tremble
as the fork lifted spaghetti
toward his lips; he wanted to go to sleep
early but not alone. He wanted to brush
his daughter's hair, and read to her,
which he did and after that began
telling her stories, simple
remembrances of growing up:
catching leopard frogs with butterfly
nets from a vernal pool that formed
in a low spot each spring in an elderly
couple's backyard; pitching pennies
against the curb of the cul-de-sac,
playing Kick-the-Can until after dark;
Perseid meteor showers; the dreamlike
aroma of bakery as he delivered
newspapers before dawn, the cold
milk and glazed doughnut
he would glide his bike downhill to,
afterward. He was glad to be lightly
tickling her back, as she had

asked him to, to be wondering
which stories she had heard,
and which ones she had missed
and when had she fallen asleep?

Assisi Heights

Time's eating them alive
on this windy hill,
the infirm and dying, these last
hundred sisters of Assisi Heights.
Ten rows of the basilica's original pews
unbolted, removed for the lineup
of wheelchairs at morning mass, a ramp
installed and painted with heavenly
swirls to match the sweeping
marble altar. No one able to plant
tulip bulbs or sow and reap the simplicity
of a vegetable garden anymore; the orchard
inherited as novitiates withered to twelve
apostolic trees, one of which is apart,
alone, somehow solitary. Each spring
on Maundy Thursday a never seen
phoenix crows three piercing times
from the tall grass under Peter's tree.
Sapphic love affairs behind closed
doors recede further into crabbed
and rotting flesh, until not even
the bitter root of a memory remains.
Wizened mouths of the deaf and blind
clamor open for torn bits of the host,
frail hands trembling like just hatched
songbirds. If we wait any longer the skulls
stretched too visible beyond these last
sisters' faces might be the last
tracks they leave on earth.

Yet just one
corporeal act of mercy in the infirmary
might make a difference tonight
as an Alberta Clipper's blizzard
winds roar out of the northwest, rattling
the convent's thousand windows; the succor
of just one pair of hands at bedside
might stanch the relentless howling, the crazed
high-pitched packs they hear singing
in rabid unison off every cornice, from every
slate roof peak, from the clatter and swirl
of branches in the diminished orchard, roused
to a manic frenzy, sprinting and yipping
up the chapel's high campanile belltower.
Tonight beneath this snowswept hill,
the South Branch of the Zumbro River rushes
through the valley of the shadow of death,
memory of the rest of the Psalmist's verses drowned
out by the wind's incessant moaning
as it rises from beside Francis, from the wolf's
likeness in the cloister's inner courtyard.
Tonight through the early solstice dark,
the enfeebled wolf of Gubbio's eyes glow
with a fierce green fire and flare
against rosaries whispered in the Chapel
of Our Lady of Lourdes, against votive shifts
of perpetual adoration, beads clutched
and stroked in the hour of death of another.
Who after these sisters sink into the earth
will bear witness should the petal-less
scent of roses perfume the air as an apparition
of the Virgin's face blossoms forth

from the chapel's roseate stone wall?
When an icon of Christ crucified
decides to speak again?
Who will beg for alms? Who will wash
Francis' uncorrupted flesh? Who will wrap
the five wounds when his stigmata reopen,
rivulets of blood trickle from his palms
to pool in the snow sifting right now
over the saint's sandaled feet?
Fur's bristling with fresh malice
along the near-starving wolf's neck
straining toward the scent of the almost
tame herd of city deer that overpopulate
the convent's grounds. Only these last
sisters can hear the frequency of cries
of another doe that has nowhere to hide
and knows it will die cornered
bleating in one of the grottos
quarried deep into the limestone
hillside. Who will bear witness
to the glazed eyes, spattered blood
curding in fresh snow, hot steam
issuing from its ripped-open guts? By dawn
it will be too late. By dawn the wolf
will resume his bloodless snarl as Francis
in his bronze rags reaches down to bless it.

Sumac Tea

one windless
feather-quiet morning
snowshoeing—trudging
through thigh deep
snow drifts   winded
catching my breath
along dense thickets
of forest-edge
sumac

supple flower heads
as if still in bloom
against winter's
desolation

white snow
brown grass
black trees

yet fresh snow glittered
stardust—points of light
sparkling in motion all around
as if celebrating something
brought back to life

reincarnated
as these sprigs
of dark red berries
curled in the shape
of each of us before birth

small enough to hold
in a father's palm

(sometimes you can break
one of your thoughts off
by its stem
place it upside down
in a jar of cold water
that turns slowly amber

then drink its mildly sweet
singularly delicious tea)

Marriage Suite

for Ellen

The happiness of the Garden that a man must lose....
—Ernest Hemingway

1. At nineteen we eased

into our canoe voyage with a river
otter's soundless glide, landed
naked in a fire-swept hillside
blueberry patch, a wild
rosebush garden ours to keep
or lose. In the hallway

as I pass you smiling in a framed
wedding pose, it's difficult
to believe there's a skeleton
lurking inside. We've witnessed
each other's changes at such
close range we need the distance
of photo albums to notice. Agape

gets the dishes washed; Eros
intervenes with Mozart
and firelight. Enmity then

peace in varying degrees,
like seasons and phases
of the moon: tonight's
full moon moist
and insistent as the nudge
of our dog's nose. Younger

we snowshoed an untrammeled
meadow of new snow
absorbing the moon. Yet can't
pretend we didn't plow that first
lovechild under for a few

more bushels of corn.

2. I applaud the just

war you wage against
nature that buries everyone's
song under the soil but

has trouble breaking down
plastic, uranium, and our
hubris. Just one microbe
on a door handle—a single
errant cell can rise,
multiply and kill. Doctors

heal by probing with myriad
little questions, while I bruise
our hearts on a couple
big ones, insisting we can recover
over a jug of Bordeaux. I keep falling

head over heels for a Montana
postcard's femme fatale
of avalanche, rattlesnake, mountain
lion and grizzly, while you're trapped
inside the world's

largest hospital, its lighted windows
posing wordless questions
through the slow blue
bleed of dawn. To that neuro

surgeon eyeballing the swag
of your tush in tight purple
scrub pants walking

the corridor, I send this cryptic
note: *Let's not*
ruin it figuring which one
of us is Cain. Married

to our bodies before birth, I
grieve my soul's eventual
loss of its shadow
hiking boot-
prints through heavy dew,
clover bone dry
an hour after sunrise.

3. Even the warm red heart of love grows

dormant and hibernates with a slowed
pulse. When our sap
flows again, we'll tap it, then boil
its faint watery sweetness
to syrup. But just now
in from the cold, the set
of your jaw and hair's wind-
scented with distance. If a child

dies before us, I'll pass
winters listening to whale
dirges from under a lake's shifting
buckling ice. Your *querencia,*

a perennial garden, September
monarchs fussing over swamp
milkweed; mine's
an old field alluvial terrace
grown up in sumac, aspen, and cedar,
where I know no matter what
I'll always be all right following my

bliss—a bird dog who flushes
a very fine meal I try not to miss
as a family covey of grouse bursts
from a thicket. Nearing the dense

high summer of our lives, so much
already behind us, yet so much
still ahead, we're no longer
able to peer very far into our over-
foliaged hearts. Even when

we die we'll never really leave
this place, no longer able to see
out from the blackness except
through our kids' eyes. I dreamt

we'll be reincarnated
as a pair of prairie
falcons nesting on Buffalo Jump
Cliff above the Yellowstone.

4. Scent of your skin that college fall

you visited lingers on the freckled
skin of this apple. In our hotel
room after a night of revelry
closing The Murray Bar
we're like children, fearless

tongues that touch
and taste everything. I remember
my crush squinting
into your face as if blinded, dizzied
by desert sunspots. More famine
in Africa, more killing
in the Middle East—the only
remedy is to find a new
path to the river then follow it
down to the waterfall where
we'll merge a few minutes

mystical and lovely as this full
lunar eclipse. Our past, petal
after petal, keeps on blooming
from the mind's rich loam,
in daydreams, even after

I throw myself headlong into
another depression: this morning
I picked wildflowers, some
courage that's yet to wilt. It's never
too late to abandon self-doubt, banish
myself forever from the bathroom
mirror. A shrink

advised me to pop florescent
blue pills, while you
ordered me to swallow a big
gulp of my pride. Instead, I ran
off into the woods with my canine
girlfriend and didn't
come back for days. No use trying
to kiss up, not after you, spitting

From now on you can just
go fuck your dog!

as I flinch
at the slap
and ricochet
of the screen door.

5. At times so in love I'm giddy imagining

you old, gray and wrinkled. Maybe someday
I'll sketch a topographical
map of your body stretched out
on the dock. Like a river's

sediments, new and old
piles of mail shift locations, as obligations
fill the calendar. Among
symptoms of boredom, Nisbet
listed: war, murder, revolution,
suicide, alcohol, narcotics,
affairs, and porn. He might
have added the erotic

heat I try to recapture from our X-
rated years. Each of my first
car's windows, a butterscotch
boat of a Chevy Malibu station
wagon, leaking in the carwash
made you laugh hysterically. A fat
paycheck won't make us happier, yet
so much easier to stare into a corral's

resplendency of sorrel
and chestnut mares. Everyday lusts
go in one eye and out
the other, while our love
leaves me blind again. I left
last night's single bourbon half-
sipped on the nightstand to prove
I'm not a lush. *Maybe*

if you helped put the kids
to bed and weren't such a goddamn
bump on the Yule
Brynner log when it comes to playing Mister
Claus, you'd get more sex,
you quipped as I fell
into a stupor.

6. Upon hearing your overseas

voice from a rowdy
Dublin pub it became a manic not dark
night of the soul. A poem's just
ink pressed into paper yet
after hearing one
of mine you hung up,
phoned back, wept, almost
forgave. Our early years

fell slow as feathers, now middle
ones plummet like a stone's
wobble to the lake bottom; eventually
we'll become the downward
drift of autumn leaf. Our moods,

like the earth's, flare
every color of the spectrum. Loneliness
like March snowmelt trickling
from the lip of the roof, barely
audible in the downspout, might

turn on a word or touch; love rise above
flood stage, then crest as during 1,001
dormitory nights. Our water

table's higher this year yet
when it isn't happening, sex
pales in comparison to what
surfaces from an underground aquifer
of consciousness, while I drive
without particular

destination, toward the sinking
red ball of winter prairie sunset, roseate
and lavender afterglow
across a frozen sea of wind-
sculpted snow and burnished grass.

7. I peer down from our bedroom

window as you kneel
faithfully tending your perennials, while
my vices like crabgrass
keep overtaking my virtues. One

late October, the twilit
undertow of the forest's ambient
glow pulls me back from the cliff,
releasing my melancholy like amber
light subsiding into forest duff.
Like the steelhead on Superior's

North Shore we make a migratory
run near winter solstice, finally turning
up the road to your parent's
glittering manor where four
generations gather like salmonids drawn to their
original beds—your girlhood
room where on Christmas early before opening
presents—our first is conceived. With a jolt

your Cabriolet sent a pregnant
whitetail airborne over the windshield, shaggy
belly fur visible overhead. A hunter
since boyhood, I felt the breathless
shudders of your chest—how your weeping
would only stop after a long
moment of regret standing graveside

in the ditch. Addressing the doe's
vacant gaze, I pressed
your palm to the unborn
fawn's soft knuckled kicks.

8. Now that I'm back cheek

to muzzle with our new pup propped
on my lap across the steering wheel, I almost
miss you risking life and limb sliding
out from your seatbelt to nuzzle. Early on,

we made a pact not to observe conspiratorial
Hallmark holidays. Instead, I leave
a sprig of sumac and a dozen frozen

rosehips on the windowsill, then sing
in praise of hunger—the Irish potato famine—
without which you'd never been born. We walked
the aisle, danced our wedding night away, and woke

the next morning a decade later. I'm still
dreaming that halcyon
summer before marriage when, alone
on the solstice, I kneel to kiss
the cold moving lips of a trout stream while you
discover a pick-your-own strawberries patch, make
jam and never live a more perfect day. How could I

not be a little attracted to your sisters, multiple
versions of your face social-
butterflying around the same room? Fireflies
blink across fresh-cut lawn, bats flutter

in a four-bourbon twilight—I'm sorry
my dick will always remain an infant
needing to be coddled and kissed. Remember
how we athletically, unwittingly starred in a live

Montana sex show for the mustachioed
man raised by a cherry picker
repairing the streetlamp through
parted curtains of our hotel window? Afterwards

you, caught your first cutthroat on a back-cast that flailed
the river while slow-moving whorls of morning
mist restored the world to its essential mystery.

9. When it snowed last night we stepped into the yard

to make another fresh start. Or is this another
dusting of white lies to cover my tracks, erase

the indulgence of where I was and why so late?
Our vows a formality, eyes teary
by the tail end of your father's
German Wedding Toast: Never let anything
or anyone build a wall between you/And may *Gott*

sei immer dir. Home from dinner and a wine we couldn't
afford, a trail of sandal on the deck, sandal
inside the door, sundress in a patch of moonlight as I mount

the stairs. On a bare island's sun-warmed boulder
surrounded by wilderness lake you made love with one eye
on the lookout over my shoulder for the Cub
Scout troop we canoed past an hour earlier. Waking

from your nightmare, a four-year old girl weeps inside
the woman I hold because her father just
hurled a wriggling, mewling burlap sack of newborn
puppies into the backyard pond. At your first cousin's

wedding, the same tawdry theme: drop kick them Jesus
through the goal posts of life. In my private religion, shafts
of cathedral-light slant down through small blue
fissures in fair-weather cumulus. Please remind—

admonish me I'm just a mammal whose needs spring
too heretically far beyond water, food, shelter. It's shamefully
easy to buy roses, much harder to clutch a pen
and nurture flowers from the void. Jubilance arrived

one sultry morning as our six-year-old son and I boogied
to *Graceland*. Whenever I crave a smoke, I'll conjure
some debonair asshole walking our daughter down the aisle.

10. On the ever-present honey-do list

of chores you tape to the fridge
each April I insist you write:
Take a long walk with me
when swales of bluebells and anemone
daub and paint the floodplain
river bottom,
as if brushed in by Monet
far as our eyes can see. At the 60th

wedding anniversary roast our three
will throw for us, I'll no doubt turn
my wizened face to yours and, cribbing
a line from that grizzled, porcine
mountain man in *Jeremiah*
Johnson, inquire: "Were it
worth the trouble, Pilgrim?" Home

from our cabin fever February
getaway to Florida, our old house
smells like fresh laundry; still drunk
on happiness, I descend the stairs
to discover pipes have burst
and flooded the basement. One irrecoverable

Indian summer day we drove
high up to winter in the snow-
capped Crazies, chopped wood, cooked a slow
elk stew then slept on lumberjack cots
beside a woodstove, swearing
we'd give up everything, someday,
to be as happy again, then drove back

down to autumn, Indian
Summer yellow and stunning
in the cottonwoods. Our present's

not safe enough
to walk on; the future muddy
and turbulent, the past flowing
dark and silent beneath
its skin of ice.

11. We'll never be as happy or fulfilled as our four

year-old sailing high
on a playground swing, but as we snuggle into bedtime
stories, she's impervious to the pure
ore of delight seeping

into our skin. Though my goose was over-
cooked long ago, winter nights I can still hold
out my hands to the warm loaves
of your body. The moment they
turned thirty-four, all my unmarried
pals envied me from their semi-
official bachelorhood, most wishing

they'd settled years ago. The year of your
promotion I became a tape
recorder selling acrylic
bathtub liners, salvaging hundreds
of poetic names for worn-out porcelain,
iron and steel: Marco Polo, Dubbini,
Jolibourg, Atlantis, Firefly, etcetera. Too many

nights our heads sink
into the pillow beside an intimate
stranger who I ask, What of all those
days fighting this intemperate
love that swings
from stifling heat to bitter
cold, if we wake
giddy and snowed in
by another blizzard
of shared sleep?

12. Older I get the less I want to clean a mess

of bluegills, go bowling, guzzle cheap
beer, beat off, or climb steep bluffs. Multifoliate
beautiful women shop Nicollet Ave. but you're the single
wildflower painting itself in profusion across swales
of river bottom, where another year's marital

bliss and transgressions wash
down into the ground with the rain. River
swollen, folk concert rained out, tent
sopped yet could you still take pity
on my blind one-eyed fish out of water
gasping for breath? When every
square inch was new, we were
as predators who swallowed their
prey whole. Twenty years later this

Sisyphus wearily rolls his marriage
boulder uphill then suddenly steps
aside to watch it crash into the river.

13. After your last harsh word knocked

the wind out of me, I drove 400
miles north to wander a forest
without apology, abandoning scars

of old logging roads for the hopeless
freedom of getting lost, determined
never to return nor ask

forgiveness for the reckless
affair I carried on in my most recurring
erotic dreams. Please stop

bitching at me about getting
our taxes done—just tell that feckless
accountant I'm out hunting
rough terrain to earn
our next meal. In a south Minneapolis

pay phone booth the end of the tunnel's
glow emanates from a Greyhound
heading nowhere into the rimrock
interior. I'm sick and tired

of you falling asleep snuggled
with a toddler, waking
like a widower to feel your side
cold and empty. Amid the gleam of my top

shelf fantasies, I'll order a glass of Juliette
Binoche, shot of Kate Winslet, snifter
of Naomi Watts, then conjure

you slipping out from the pale
chrysalis of your raggedy-assed
nightgown.

14. Let's measure our wealth in wine

aging in a makeshift cellar, shelves
stuffed with vintage books, wild game
in the freezer waiting to bestow
its wildness. Are we the only ones

in America dining on tapas of fondued
prairie chicken, middle course of grilled
snipe and woodcock, entrée of Alice B.
Toklas' braised grouse? With your hair cropped

short, splendidly dominant
nose and boyish face, I can almost
mistake you for a Left Bank
lesbian, or David of bedtime
Bible story fame. Once upon a time
the night was always still young
and so were we, who now
pass out sober slurring
Mother Goose. Early

to bed with a new
novel, glass
of Bordeaux and soft
chafe of your stubbly
Shangri La.

15. A pool of blood

and afterbirth, your perineum
ripped and lower
half shaking like a hypo-
thermic bird dog—as that
doctor asshole who kept
calling from his golf cart
before he showed to suction
out our posterior son, turned
and quipped: *Don't*
fret, a few
stitches and she'll
be good as new. I wince

and cry out as you tweeze
a sliver, dig
pitilessly deeper mocking
my frenetic contortions: *Men are*
so pathetic; I gave
birth to your daughter without
lidocaine or an epidural. Suck it up,
wimp. You press

my hand to the drum-
tight hump of your belly, the muscled
pulse of a miniature foot, *Eine Kleine*
Nachtmusik without the distraction
of sound. Swift and terrible

as crow shadows descending
the windshield, the déjà vu
I've driven away from the little

guy stranded on the driveway in his
plush car seat, my panic leaping
into the rearview. Pregnant, your

face held my gaze, the first pastel
blush of spring in the hardwoods, as we
thrilled to just budded
fingers and toes in the monitor, a tiny
heartbeat's steady patter. Your belly

grew into a battle of tubers
and roots, a giant
milkweed pod swelling
with juice and silk, gall
engorging goldenrod
stems. First days

home with our newborn, we were high
on an Indian summer elixir
of cool breeze and warm sun blending
against our skin—until a squall

out of the northwest ripped
autumn from the trees, rain lashing
the panes as the phone rang and rang
until we woke to a bassinet's
wailing: Your grandpa
wouldn't survive the night.

16. As the dog dashes toward a flotilla

of wintering geese that lift off
honking all at once, my scalp
prickles with false
satori as these messengers only
trumpet my dull worrying
from a park bench. Naive and too

young we married purely
for love, yet I've made you rich
in agates, arrowheads and fossils. A penniless
backslider, I'm making a reverse
commute against a current
of headlights to repatriate the skull
of a red fox, a bald eagle's
illegal tailfeathers, the papery
globe of a wasp nest. How can I

go on regarding the future as if
it were the local forecaster's worse
case scenario—a terrible
derecho? Reading
a novel at the wheel
on Nebraska's interstate, I imagine

my successor as wealthy and debonair,
a GQ sophisticate, interested
in opera, polo, dueling pistols. So

kick me once hard in the ass with a pointed
high heel as a reminder not to live
waiting for something to happen
that never does. Kick me, twice.

17. Stranded by a swollen river's

muddy torrent, no matter how
far upstream or down I walk
in this dream of death, I can't
find a way to cross to you—your lips
move though I can't hear
what you're saying on the opposite
bank. On a mission not to die,

suddenly aware how heaven's
revealed to us all along
whenever we meditate upon flowers,
birds, rivers, the tidal drift of stars. On this
harvest moon, is it true that only

married love wanes until it's less
than nothing then waxes
toward fullness again?—even as this old
wooden drift boat of our years scrapes
to a halt on dry cobble, detritus
from past floods snagged
high in riparian branches. I woke

to your palm warm on my
fontanel, your other hand
on the dog's brow in an equal
blessing of hair and fur.

18. Please scatter my ashes off the Lake

Mary dock saving a handful
each for Superior and the Mississippi,
so from my home watersheds
I can join three oceans, a dead
bloom, the Gulf Stream, and keep
circling the globe. Or just

bury me St. Francis-style, blue
and naked in raw earth, at the edge
of a birch copse in the last
row of worn and lichened
stones in that hidden pioneer
cemetery, my skull
resting within earshot
of the tumult of grouse, their miniature
sonic booms. On Memorial Day

you might split open
one's packed crop and place
its blossoming contents—clover,
acorn, aspen bud, birch catkin—
at my headstone. We fledge

this final nest alone, our family
perched around whispering,
It's okay to go: If I ever
need a shove, please remember
how compassion forced us to
the same for our dogs. And sweep

a shock over my widow's
peak bald spot.

19. Any moment I could stroll down and board

that Greyhound to another
life. Half diseased, a decade
came and went as we searched
for a cure to slow time. Surely someday,

as soon as tomorrow, we'll quit
our jobs, put the house
on the market, pull the kids
from school, zero out
every account and move to an abandoned
farmstead just outside Beach,
North Dakota—where—living free
at the end of a gravel road
and clear off the interest indefinitely—we'll hoist

three bundles onto our backs and watch
them grow into joyful
burdens. What I want most is to be
able to write as freely as our son
finger-paints, though it's more often
than enough to imagine my non
musical hands strumming the length
of your body. In the scar

of an elm where a major
limb was sawed, I can see a tribal
mask, theatre's tragic
frown, Christ's passion, the strain
of your face in childbirth, Courbet's
Origin of the World—or just another
Penthouse pussy painting? I stared
for months through a kitchen window

unable to see beyond my nose.
After reading Anne Frank, I decided
to draw the curtain on self-pity, all
inconsequential despair. Despite steep

odds in this land of icehouse lights, mounted
bucks, big-trout contests and billboard
fetuses, I have passed like a bull
moose through the eye
of a needle, so that as an Alberta

Clipper blows heavy across the borderline,
we lounge naked in a cabin window's
pool of woodstove warmth, braiding strands
of each other into ourselves
supple as rope. What are these

thousands of little
deaths we've shared if not preparation
for the cosmic flameout to star-
dust at the very end?

20. Like the river that thaws

then freezes back over with a film
of slush, I'm blurred and indecisive
about another baby. Before

sunrise our city's the faint
coo and gurgle of pigeons roosting
in girders under a footbridge, street
lamps like our intimacy clicking
imperceptibly on and off. Among the homeless,

I beg for words, the weight of moldy
hay in an abandoned barn, to build slow
heat for decades until a cache
spontaneously combusts. St. Francis
kissed such lepers and loved

creation so much he demanded to be
buried naked in wormy earth. I want to believe
all souls will be drawn together then raised up
like flocks of autumn blackbirds
streaming as one ceaseless wave
from the tallest cottonwood—yet this steady

downpour of the heart won't let up
until your plane lands and I inhale
ocean, sunburn, Santa
Ana winds. After long absence, the first

touch is tentative, fingertips
like dragonflies just skimming
the lake surface. Patches of snow

trillium in bloom, white-
throated sparrow's treetop *O-oh*
sweet Canada, Canada, Canada,
long circular wail
of mating loons—we're back
up north, far from city lights,
to find out whether dimmed love
can renew itself the way the stars
pulse with starlight again.

21. As I practice T'ai Chi Chih, you

and the kids, engrossed
in another board game, ignore
my flowing limbs, my mind purling
with riparian light
until I'm less than nothing
special. Without a book

entering the high
summer of life, I'll keep
walking these late-
blooming fields of aster
and goldenrod, to bring you fragrant
bouquets in our early
fall. In the morning

as I walk the riverbank
of my thoughts, I write
like the dickens, never more
frenzied than while immersed
through the window in rain
or snow—wide, hypnotic,
vertical rivers flowing down
from the sky. Deeper into this

westward journey, the faint
outline of a mountain range appears
still far in the distance. When it looms
I'll ask to be carried up to a not-
very-secret medicine hole. As earth-
cooled air blows through the thin
veil of my body, I'll wake
on the other side loping

an Appaloosa toward
the promised campfire—where I'll brush
the orchard of our unborn
daughter's hair, damp
with moonlight.

22. Years ago, you caught the breeze

blowing out from my gaze, trembling
like a single outlying aspen
against the stillness of a hillside
forest. Those peerless

hours of reading in a canvas tent—
it rained three days straight—
when your face
first blinded me to time, are peerless
because they'll only happen
once. Our first

time was no miraculous
parting Red Seas; my gently combing
fingers then tongue probed a lovely
pink mollusk. One night I dreamt

a perfect sonnet you scrawled
across a restaurant napkin,
but as I woke the words
evaporated like invisible ink, my lips
still mumbling their cadence. I started too

young with stolen sips; my liver's
odometer's already
turned over once, yet donate
my 20/20 and all salvageable
organs. Please, O gods, don't

send disease or a fatal storm. Our sap's
still rising, our bloom not yet gone.

If you go first, I promise to keep
a vigil, weeping like Magdalene
at her lover's nailed feet. Just before

the shovel's first blind
thud on your casket, I'll raise
the lid to kiss your wan
horribly cold,
sewn lips.

23. That we owe God a death

might grant us an inviolate
freedom to go and love
at any moment
whomever we wish: Mondays
at the gym I imagine the same
yoga instructor's tanned thighs
wrapped around my face, inhale
her cypress
swamp's sweet musk. Our sex

life of late like junk food
when famished, just calories, faux
meat patty I grab from a Kwik
Trip to fill my gut. Whatever
happened to nights of filet

mignon so tender we wanted
each morsel to last? Not
in the mood again, then selflessly
so I can pretend thou art
a neighbor's wife. In my recurring

dream of a wedding party that's
endless with more and new brides-
maids arriving, more champagne
on trays floating the parquet
electric with trysts—yet one

whiff of your sweaty perfumed
neck I'm raring—delighted
to leave the strobe and throb

of townhall dance floor fading
as you lead

me out by the wrist, bare
feet ticklish through
lush summer grass, to a Holstein
pasture's lone burr oak, into the soft

tender aura of miniature
violets on your sundress—my tongue
plunged into the delirium
between your pale, freckled thighs,
renewing my vows to your divine
perineum that vanishes

into a toddler's elbow in my ribs, harsh
chirp of crickets, brawling
sparrows, your light
obnoxious snore.

24. Tipsy

at a college party you quipped
to my pals: *He's got a gigantic*
forehead, huge hands, big feet, but doesn't
swing a thick stick! Long distance

by phone I could identify subtle
or strident gradations in your mood
like birding by ear—song sparrow, oriole,
agitated house wren, onerous blue jay,
balmy yellow warbler by day; mockingbird,
mourning dove, whip-poor-will
at night when I spared you from

blonde, blue-eyed, wickedly
handsome Jim with his San Diego weather
and missionary—his sunny 70 degrees
of stasis—bland as a communion wafer—
while I, speaking in tongues of metaphor,
turned you on with figurative

milk of the waxing moon—theory
and practice of counting down
sleeps—until the body of the other
waxed into fullness the moment
you stepped from a plane. Waltzing

down the runway, into my pre
9/11 arms at the gate, our
once-in-a-blue—sometimes blood—

moon embrace. Tender were the nights
of finger-and-toenail-trimmed
love already waning gibbous to slenderest
crescent the morning you suddenly left

us both in tears again—no moon
which was a new moon I dreaded
on the other side of the country
in the middle of our long absence. Often

in a fit of contrition
rather than pique, I confessed
my most egregious sins—yet secret,
small things I could never tell, still
come and go like ants: Late adolescent

infatuated with you, I half-
believe nubile girls with alabaster
skin could not possibly
poop and almost stay
doped on my illusion for years—until

the morning after I popped
the question, sick
from Amoxicillin, you swerve
off a Wyoming interstate, leap
into the ditch, gushing forth
as I lovingly swab
your bare legs.

25. No Tall Pine God

to keep us safe, just this remnant
white pine stand an Ice
Age left behind to stay
dry under while fishing. En route,

we witness the split
second difference
between the bounding white
flag of an alarmed doe's safe
crossing and her fawn
smeared across asphalt, reek
of a pulp mill overwhelming
our jalopy as we enter a grim

outpost of the far
north punctured by a tavern's
neon arrow blinking a fifty
fifty chance of fistfight. Zipped
inside a mummy
bag, captive under night's tidal
drift of stars, I'm too

wary of all the ways we might
be killed—and only
relax as we paddle
toward the shimmering magenta
dot of civilization that'll haul us
back toward our drab
routine of lunch in the hospital

cafeteria. Through the ER, then
the cancer ward, an elevator up to the neo-
natal ICU, I wait by a window
of tiny feet, incubator
tubes, grateful as you bend
to tie your shoe we're this
far and still alive.

26. We shoved off from a crowd

of well-wishers gathered— receding—then
dispersing from the dock, after which
I rowed us in circles for years around
my latent desire for a quick
buck and a mistress's
imaginary allure. Surely I forgot

to become a know-it-all
doc or shyster, instead mumbling English
Major during job interviews with hot
flashes of self-consciousness, while the book
shop I conceived in the shadow
of a double-decker Barnes & Noble grew
more doomed from the start. My only
marginal success: this self-

induced non-paying labor of peering out
at the world while staring
into my heart at the same time. One eye
catches you in close
quarters, enchanted
as you step from the shower; the other
tries to follow as you hustle
down the sidewalk then disappear
through a row of pines that signals
the start of your shift inside the world's
largest hospital—my inner
eye blindsided, negative
capability nonplussed. Mistakes swarm

my head like deer flies I try
to crush as another drills
its stinging welt. Last then first

names fade until only a dim
face remains, yet I knew the inner
contours of these women
over whom reveries bloom like spring
ephemerals I want
shaded out by the canopy
of our union. Together let's

cut loose this anchor
rope and drift
free from every
notion of divorce.

27. Just inside Yellowstone we sunk

into the sublime pleasures of a thermal
creek as flash floods at home
swept seven from highways
the week of the county fair. Kids ride carved
horses to calliope, as even the saddest
adults stare vaguely smiling. Bored,

I slowly circle you naked, prodding
like a cattle judge, here and there. At
the outset of our mosquito-bitten
voyage, you insisted on grandeur
of the South Pacific; me jobless, we
settled for Superior, our cold
inland sea—unaware how

far across or how deep below—
we survived peering through rose-
colored glasses long after we knew
we were wearing them. On a nameless
lake, whipped by whitecaps, without
you as ballast, I fear this refurbished
scow of my middle years will
surely capsize. If we've settled

into each other like an old
Victorian, discover a new life
you never want to leave—try on a new
personality lain dormant within you
so long you forgot it exists. Then fall
in love with it, yet don't give
credit to the person whose touch
or voice unearths it. Too proud

of this wild forest chicken I stalked
in cold sleet to snap-shoot once
through pines and not miss, I prance
the kitchen in a wine-buzzed
victory lap. The dishes

can wait: Somehow, in greasy apron
and chef's hat, I've earned
your pleasures tonight, down

by this fire of applewood.

28. Darling, how is it you never

tire of G. Keillor, our secular
bishop's treacly
high-pitched tremolo and twangy
choir, his woe-begone
homilies that drudge me to sleep? Dozing

after evening mass, over a cabernet
and *Saturday Night Live*, as your shin
brushes my calf, I grow sad
for my priest friend, Father Tom, an ex-
farm boy who wishes he could marry
not burn. Your grandfather's
footprints prance across the lake,
the wind's pathways glittering
ascension light. If the Church is one

big circus tent's death-
defying act, a high-wire faith
without nets, years ago I lost
my ticket yet keep sneaking in
under a loose stake. Your New

Testament heart thuds its Good
News into my rib cage, but only King
Sol's prenups can oxygenate
my blood. Despondent

in early winter, bent on disappearing
at gunpoint, what saves me is a thin
mist of citrus grazing my cheek

as you peel a Texas
ruby grapefruit.

29. Like a sundial

we slowly turn away
until we're in cold shadow
then inch back toward
one another's warmth. Home

from my canoe trip, your limbs
are strong as water rippling its moist
light over the light-grey skin
of shoreline cedars. You in your perennial
gardens, me following my bird dog's wake
through the morning woods, we separate
like a braided creek, yet remain
one creek all the way upstream
and one all the way down. This
wooden boat of our years doesn't leak
with its fresh coat of paint
and little repairs. We close

the cabin in fall, leaving the stereo on,
and return in spring to music
that's reveled in itself all winter.

30. In intervals, our marriage measured

in dog years, which one
we loved at the time, and how
long we had her. I'll bury Rose under a pioneer

family's picnic oak on Melchior
Ridge above Whitewater Valley's early morning
shroud then mark her grave with a bouquet
of red-phase grouse feathers. All thirty-three

windows of our first house leaked
yet their arctic whistling soothed
a newborn. The first night you left
me alone I proffered a desperate male
nipple to stall his crying. Now a boy

and girl chase a yellow
Lab pup through a sprinkler across lush
green shining grass and the dream
of which I am unaware as we live it
grows more aware of us. On bitter nights,

Rose asleep at the foot of our bed, feet tucked
beneath her ribs for extra warmth, an aura
of grace slips between us. Dogs

like kids tempt my patience until
I reject—I regret the trajectory of my hand
cocked to deliver
its hurt. From feisty puppy to greying
muzzle, Rose tethers our kids
to a future of sudden grief, unaware the joy
they kiss trots toward oblivion. In the North-

woods she leads me down the trail
of my thoughts, translating the creature
world with her nose, then curls
on our bunk, eyelids and paws twitching
with grouse dreams. If only I could

absorb this moment-by-moment world
with the exhilaration of a dog's
muzzle out the passenger window, nostrils
seining the wind.

31. Across the street in Saint Francis

Peace Garden I stroll the buffer—limestone
grotto, Norway's profligate
spruce, rows of deciduous
like Cezanne's *Chestnuts*
at Jas de Bouffan, rushing
fountain, falls and cascading
stream, shimmer of
pennies in reflection pools—that
keeps despair at bay between
our bat-infested shack
and the Generose psyche ward
aka looney bin. What journalist

schmuck could have ever conjured
poetry as North America's most
dangerous occupation, with poets dead
last in life expectancy? Show me a workman's
comp form for writer's
block or the tunnel
vision of depression, one day
of PTO for Percy's reentry

problem. As hours of writer's sweat wicks
from my armpits, only a single phrase bleeds
through my forehead. Rejoicing
in the comforting stench of my dirt
poor poet pals, I'm mindful the only true
aristocracy is consciousness. A little
coffee or nicotine sharpens
the instrument while bourbon
blunts then grinds
it to a stub. Years

of early morning meadow
and forest walks have carried me
far from the nearest
noose, into my mind's
invincible summer, all shadow
yet sunshot with the swaying

light of words.

32. The pheasant I crippled with a Hail

Mary lost in cornrows, my ace
bird dog searching as the red
ball of sun sinks into oaks blackened
by regret. I'm heading where

ever this aimless Midwestern
diligence takes me, quite often
to Char's Dogpatch, tavern
with a trout stream, strippers
and a jukebox. Sorry, Love, but

Marlo, your girlhood hero, was wrong: This
land is neither yours nor mine, but rather
that farmer's whose forebears
got here first then booted
the Dakota out. When the sky

hailed golf balls, we gunned
your Cabriolet for an abandoned
pole-barn, where all our old
complaints against each other battered
a tin roof. So humid

last night I dreamt
my legs straddled
the continent, one Paul
Bunyan foot in each
cool ocean surf. What we need
is an undertow—a rip
tide of will to turn

the other cheek, ship
the kids off to summer camp, then turn
this silver key
and split.

33. February bird dog bored

and horny unfaithfully humps the neighbor
kid's knee. Squirrels multiply
their tracks, relentless
low dirge-clouds bury the shed
antler of a new moon. Samsara,

the seasons, and your endless
cycle of unpacking another
holiday's kitsch. O Lover

of Lamps, our new bedside
beauty burns too high and hurts
your blue eyes, while another low-
hovering Mayo ER chopper rattles
the windows and weakens
our mortar. First crack

of dawn turns crusted, muted
snow lavender as the scent
of your neck, yet my heart's
flush with the little dooms
slanting down from each
fence post. An oxidized

film and overwintering pod of spent
fruitflies floats on the *Domaine
Tempier Bandol*
we sipped and wasted over last
night's argument: So what if

I chug this bitter
vinegar down to bits

of crumbled cork? As late winter
dusk wraps itself around the hill, this
buffalo-robed Sisyphus easily
shoulders the rising
Full Sap Moon.

34. I only meant to have a long

look around, fish then leave
at daybreak. A decade later, the town-
ship road closed by flood, staring
into the same brown water, I'll never flee

this upland of corn and soybeans,
dendritic with trout streams, or plunk
the daydream of my canoe in the plunge
pool below the Power Dam and drift
my way down to New Orleans. Wise as a kid,

I gradually grew
dumb, dumber—dumbest as a well-
educated gent of thirty-three pining for
a life beyond our game-
trail hikes through autumn
sumac. Should I ever stop

myself from believing that every raptor
soaring low over the windshield's a sign
something wonderful or very
grave's about to happen? After the monotony

of church and quarreling
children, sweaty from mowing, I flip
through a comic book
Kama Sutra seeking a new
way to enthrall our limbs. In the month

of county fairs, we're stalled at dusk
with a jolt at the Ferris-wheel's

peak of the year, suspended as close
as we'll get to paradise
above the Republic's ramshackle
farmsteads and small town
water towers blinking an infinite

Yes, my palm on the blade
of your shoulder while Venus
lights itself, one lamp
over the rumpled prairie.

Lost in the Art of Poetry

Is this the same log fallen across the same
creek I've crossed a dozen times,

am crossing, and will cross
again, without start or finish?

Upstream, I can't see into the snow-
blurred future, nor downstream very

far into the past. I try to keep
my balance: each bank

a beginning and end, neither
one nor the other. The current

flows in its ceaseless
present in which my reflection tries

to outpace the shortness of life. I cross
the creek, wander through spruce

and undifferentiated aspen, and after
a while wander back, but my tracks

that keep arriving from both
directions, the ones I've followed

fade, along with daylight in the pure
silence of falling snow, where

it is a hundred years from now,
and I am dead, and someone else

is here, far from home in fear
of the time until morning, a form

absorbing the silence of his grave,
alone in the darkness, listening.

Sweat Lodge

5:15
Inside Dan Abraham Healthy Living Center
Men's steam room the atmosphere's
A sweat lodge
Where I'm naked among
Members of my tribe

5:16
The patterned tiles gleam
Pastels polished
Smooth as river stones
Six walls facing our six
Sacred directions dripping
In beaded condensation
A hot steady rain
Of fine droplets
The scalding
Cairn of river rocks
Long since removed
(For the sake of safety)
From center of the floor
Replaced by stainlesssteel drain
The source of our sacred
Fire beyond a mysterious
Vent now issuing a hissing spume
Of geyserhot steam each time our sacred
Firekeeper concealed in an utility
Closet beyond the south wall pours

With a hollowed-out wooden scoop
Cold piped riverwater we hear scorch
The pulsing red heat of the stones

5:19
A long continuous hiss
And moan of steam in fissures
That last until our tireless
Firekeeper out of pity finally halts
The barrage with a sudden
Automatic click
As if our steam is set on a timer
A mechanized switch that ushers in
A deep primordial hush
Dense floor-to-ceiling whorls
So thick I can only make out the faintest
Outline of members of my tribe
An apparition of faces
That shifts in and out of focus
A silence so pure
It's from an ancient time
Before the ancient hymns
Before the ancient choirs
Before even the first word
Spoken by the first man
Steam so thick it stifles breath

5:20
In the hours before dawn we gather
During our lunch breaks we gather
Before and after work we gather
In this pristine heat and fluid

My tribe enduring
The line between pain and pleasure
To float free of our cares
Until one by one as a tribe we emerge
From the amniotic dark
Facing the sun's
Eternal rebirth
Back into the light of the world
As if gasping for first breath
Our skin supple
Infantsoft and new
Tingling as we emerge
From this living symbol
Our Mother Earth's sacred womb

5:23
My tribal brothers
In science and medicine
Come and go
Yet without prayers
Without offerings of tobacco
Or red cedar incense
Without medicine bundles
For we are not Indians
Not *Mdewakanton*
Not *Wahpekute*
Not *Santee*
Not *Lakota*
Not *Hunkpapa*
Nevertheless we're not quite
Fully *Wasichus* either
We're almost something

Else while immersed in the steam
My tribe's sweat lodge
Almost a true sweat lodge
Except for the dim light
Of incandescent bulbs
Glowing from metal
Safety cages
A digital clock
That displays time's
Harsh red numbers
Brutal tick-tock
So nobody stays in too long
So that my tribe of healers
Will always be on time for work
A true sweat lodge
Would be dark as inside a cave
Except for a pulsing cairn of river stones
And tip of the peace pipe as it's passed
Hand-to-hand
Like a floating ember

5:26
A true sweat lodge
Would smell of wood
And tobacco smoke
Be round as an image
Of the circle of life
Not square
Not this cube of hard
Edges and lines
Grouted ceramic tile
Its frame woven

Of peeled willow sapling
Bowed and lashed
With deer or bison
Sinew
Wigwam-style
Domed walls
And roof a pungent
Weave of pine
And cedar boughs
Mudded with clay
Cache of moccasins
Outside the swift
Zumbro River current
A barely audible whisper

5:27
And there would not now be circulating in our steam
An antiseptic congress of egotism
Nor hubris
Nor arrogance
Nor God Complex
But these are the mark of my tribe
Occupational hazards
Of those doing the near-miraculous
Work of my tribe
Best of the brightest men of medicine
Whose collective genius hour-by-hour
Tips the balance between death and life
Surgeons whose dexterous hands perform
Earthly miracles for this famous Clinic
At great personal risk
Of physician's Black Lung Disease

This big problem among my tribal brethren
To become addicted to the belief
That one knows nearly everything
About almost anything
Such as horses
Such as hunting
Such as native wildflowers
Such as fine art
Such as French wine
Such as classical music
Such as Shakespeare
Nor would my tribal brethren
After they step from the steam
Stare with admiration into mirrors
Overpleased by their own visages
Nor in the privacy of their grand tepees
Treat their squaws as receptacles
For semen and jobstress

5:29
But this is my tribe
This is my tribe with whom for better
And for worse I have lain down my roots
My tribe seeking surcease
From its worries here in the steam
In one of the world's famous places
Where peoples from all ends
Of the earth, from all walks and from every
Nation on earth arrive in jets
In search of healing
Far too many for freedom
From fear of immanent death

Here in this world
Famous mecca for the medical arts
Where people of all creeds and religions
Of all colors and all cultures
Gather in one place
Under one roof mingling
Huddled together in the same waiting rooms
Just as warring tribes in earlier times
Gathered all across the West
Where it was agreed by mutual consent
There would be no fighting
Over the flow of healing waters
Among enemies soaking
At the hot springs

5:31
The Dali Lama was just here
Preaching peace
Many Great Fathers from Washington have come here
Hollywood comes here
Lou Gehrig was diagnosed here
Cortisone was discovered here
JFK was here as a teenager for his chronic back
(Cutting – it is still rumored – a wide
Swath through the surfeit of single nurses)
Hemingway was electroshocked just down
And across the street from my house
At the world's largest hospital
Where my wife works
The great author's temples rubbed with grease
His memory swiftly erased
As he bit down on the thick rubber mouthpiece

Gerald Ford came here just before he passed
Ronald Reagan before he loped off
To the Happy Hunting Grounds
Bill Clinton dedicated this shine
Our new employee fitness center
Our tribe's sacred sweat lodge
Charles Lindbergh, Helen Keller, Roy Rogers
FDR at the height of his powers
All guests of the Brothers Mayo
Great Chiefs Will and Charlie
Today's *Post-Bulletin* says Saudi King
Jumbo jets transporting his entourage
Will soon be landing
At this great and important hub on earth
To which people of great means
Along with the poorest of the poor
Arrive together as refugees and pilgrims
To check into the edifice of our Clinic
Too often as a last desperate search for help
All united by hope
We pray to be healed
By the grace of the Great Spirit
Through the integrated councils
And dance of collective genius
Of my tribe of holy men and women
Amen

5:34
Our team of doctors of great renown
All of whom breathe a long sigh
Of release here in the steam
Surgeons mingling with nurses

Chief financial officers with orderlies
All seeking respite from the weight
Of their cares in the purifying
Heat of the steam
Relief from the invisible
Pall that hangs like an inversion
In the air over the shallow valley of my tribe
Fine particulates
Soot of death and disease
Settling in our lungs like coal dust

5:36
We let it seep from our pores
Here in the steam
We purge ourselves
Here in the steam
We build up a little immunity
Here in the steam
Before we step out
From the sanctuary of our sweat lodge
Back into the trenches
Of our species' long and ongoing
War without beginning or end
My tribe of healers having counted
Coup many times on our enemies
My tribe of warriors having won
Many skirmishes since our forebears
Broke this prairie sod
My tribe of innovators having forged
New kinds of weaponry and armor
A logo of three overlapping shields

Patient Care
Education
Research
In order that we might
Lose this war ever more slowly
So that those already cut down
As our tribe's great shaman
Will Mayo once
Thundered pounding his podium
Shall not have died in vain

5:37
I am in reverie here in the steam
In reverie over my tribe's origins
In reverie over its humble roots
I am proud here in the steam
How this great city rose up
How this sprawling campus rose up
From nothing
From the middle of cornfields
To flourish
On the windswept prairies
Where the buffalo
And nomadic Dakota once roamed
Until my tribe moved in
With its plows and oxen
Its silos and corncribs
To break the raw prairie sod
To erect this improbable monolith
I am sweating in reverie
Amid a fresh onslaught of steam

5:38

Strong medicine of the steam
Sear and hiss of steam
Almost a serum to breathe
A scythe inside the chest
Heads draped ghostly under towels
Dizzy with the heat
Some gasping for breath
Some fleeing our sweat lodge
The future of my tribe in doubt
The price of our healing work is high
The costs take their toll
My people tired yet well-fed
My people rich yet stressed
My people weary of meetings
My people living in perpetual fear
Of productivity reports
Medicare reimbursement
Endless documentation
Wrath and scrutiny
Of insurance companies
The great ongoing morass
Of health care reform
Everyone his own shaman
Seeking his vision here in the stream
Every idea big or small
Evaluated by a system of sub-tribes
One committee merging into another
In order to help our tribe
Stay solvent
As council by council we chant
We chant our scared mission

The needs of the patient come first
Even as we sacrifice
Even as we sweat and drip
Toward temporary release
The saving remnant of a vision
That may never arrive
In the rank heat of our steam

5:39
Who is our sacred fire
Keeper no one's ever seen
Year by year more
Mysterious beyond his wall
Guardian of my tribe's sacred texts
My tribe's earliest pictographs
Scrawled on limestone
Bricks quarried from ancient
Semitropical shallow seabeds
Some believe he's a spirit
Risen from the dead
That if you had a key
You'd find no bones
Just an empty tomb
I imagine a woodshed
At one end of his spacious
Utility closet
From the other the gush
Of a giant spring
I among my tribesmen
All of us sweating for a vision
Amid the bliss
And agony of the steam

Delirious in the steam
Solemn in the steam
Back to the Dream Time
Survey markers still fresh
Hatchet marks fresh
In section-corner oak saplings
Land with the dew still on it
A Peaceable Kingdom
Virgin sod black as the coal
A prairie wildflower garden
Through which the founder of our tribe
Sailed by Conestoga wagon
Arriving here as an inspector
Of copper mines
River ferry pilot
Yeoman farmer
Part-time doctor sometimes
Treating a sick horse
Until a war-time summons
Enchanted drumbeat
From the Supreme Chief
In distant Washington
Abraham Lincoln

5:41
Now the Great Uprising
Now the slaughter of innocents
Our women and children forced to flee
To hide for days in cattail sloughs
Raped and scalped
Our women to take up pitchforks
To tuck their hair in and pose

Like men going into battle
The founder of my tribe
Treating the freshly wounded
The Little Doctor
Barking swift orders
In a saloon surrounded by siege
Deep in this land
That was not quite our land
From sea to shining sea
Until our Council of Chiefs
In the capitol of St. Paul
By order of our mightiest fort
The White House
In far-off Washington
Sent troops
To quell and vanquish
To expel and banish
To secure our borders
To separate friend from foe
To harass and punish
To chase and skirmish
To root out and arrest
These enemy combatants
One nation
Under the Great Spirit
Indivisible
With mass execution for all

5:43
Shakopee and Big Eagle hanged
Mankato bludgeoned by cannonball
Little Crow shot in the back raspberry-picking

Red Cloud deported to rot on his reservation
Crazy Horse bayoneted in the kidney
Sitting Bull turned into a cartoon character
Chief Seattle chased and skirmished
Harassed and hunted to exhaustion
The last cut down in the snows
Last of the Ghost Dancers
Starving, mad, hysterical
Cut down by Gatling gun
With Chief Big Foot
Limbs akimbo
Frozen in bloodsmeared
Snow at Wounded Knee

5:44
In the steam the hooves
Of history paw and tamp the earth
In the stream a trader's
Mouth stuffed with ants and grass
In the steam settler children
Each with a pitchfork
Thrust through the forelock
In the steam the scream of arrow
Wounds flushed with whiskey
In the steam wriggling papooses
Bayoneted in the temple
A stained beard dripping
Tobacco juice, big dumb
Laugh Nits make lice
In the steam a thousand ponies
Swoop down in a pageantry
Of face paint and eagle feathers

Thunder and dust
In the steam a vast white garment
Stretched across the prairies
Of southern Minnesota
Saturates with blood

5:46
In the steam 38 Dakota sing from nooses
Blindfolded they sing
(Can you hear them sing?)
Draft horses spurred then whipped
The platform rips away
Feet kicking until they jerk
Wildly then dangle
To a listless halt
In cloak and tunic
The doctors arrive by lanternlight
To haggle over cadavers
One called Cut Nose
His carcass dismembered
Tossed down an outhouse hole
Retrieved from the dung
By the founder of my tribe
The short-statured horse-and-buggy
Doctor who started all this
Whose unborn sons would lead us
Whose sons would become surgeon
Whose sons would become shaman
Whose sons would become legend
Whose sons would learn anatomy
From a kettle of bones
Articulating the skeleton

That hung in our Founding Father's study
Archived scalp and tanned skin of this
Hanged Red Man an impossible
Conundrum and perpetual gift
For the advancement of modern medicine
From the greatest of our Great White Fathers
In far-off Washington
Whose pocked and craggy face
Stares forever east from Paha Sapa
Across Great Plains
Over Killdeer Mountain
Over Whitestone Hill
Toward Birch Coulee
Toward New Ulm
Toward Fort Ridgley
Toward Wood Lake
Toward Montevideo
Toward Camp Release
Toward Mankato
Toward Fort Snelling
Toward Rochester
Dynamited into the side of a mountain
Staring forever in the direction of my tribe
Staring as so few can into his tribe's heart
Into his own heart
Out into the fallen world
At the same time
Staring until the end of human time

5:51
I am in reverie here in the steam
Over my tribe's origins in the steam

Naked among my gifted and talented
My world-renowned tribe of healers
Who devote long hours
Overtime without pay
Who labor in spare time writing papers
Who rise without complaint
All hours of sleepless nights
To beeping pagers
Who give their whole lives over
Who give their personal cell numbers over
I am in awe and reverie here in the steam
My tribe of healers soaking
Away their cares in the steam
Where out of good manners
And Midwestern reserve
And Minnesota Nice no one speaks
Where one rarely speaks in the sacred
Moments of purifying oneself
In the never-ending surcease of the steam

5:53
Ah, yes, our antiseptic-scented steam
Same as the steam of the ancients
Chanting words from a different time
Naked in the steam of thermal creeks
Our steam the same as their steam
As steam rising from fumaroles
Across the geyser basins of Yellowstone
Steam no different than Rocky Mountain steam
Sacred stream rising from the great mineral
Hot springs of Thermopolis, Wyoming
Steam of purest boiling spring water

Yes, the journey of my tribe of healers
Begins and ends just west of the Mississippi
Where my tribe has everything it needs
Here in the bluff valleys of the Zumbro
One fine morning my tribe will awake
One day here in the stream inside our cramped
Sweat lodge inside the men's locker room
Of the Dan Abraham Healthy Living Center
One day my tribe will leave this world
And dream itself back to reality

God and Art

for Betsy Sholl

No one will ever really understand this
world made by a god that can create
an eagle yet can't construct an aerie,
an eagle's immense stick nest;
that after 250 million years still gives
rise to the human world yet can't write
a sonnet, compose opera, or sketch
a nude, still life, or landscape.
Though as Courbet, before walking
off in a huff, once quipped to a party
of highbrow artists: *See that sunset
out the window? No one will ever
be as good as God*—for whom
the light so many struggle
to capture with paint or words
effortlessly creates its own magnificence.

Myth of the Aerie

All summer
the parent eagles worked
a hidden bay of this reservoir for dead
panfish and bass afloat on the surface,
food they've reared their nestling on,
who has learned to fish the way I fished
with Dad and ate his catch. In those days
I blindly pledged allegiance to the flag
and only saw eagles on fishing
trips to the far north, its lakes
and pine-scented air a reprieve
from endless row crops, the fetor
of hog farms, from DDT thinning
their eggshells to the point they almost
ceased to exist. In those days
a hundred-dollar bill was a sight
to behold, and the aggressive ferocity
of bald eagles went unquestioned.

§

At twilight, as this family of three
perched in silhouette at the far
end of the bay passes and eats
their fish supper—as I drift
my canoe under a towering
white pine waiting for these
shadowy figures to glide
back to their immense stick nest,
the Republic for which they stand
seems far away even as the sound
of its traffic rises from a highway,

while the mystery of the child
who is father to the man
draws infinitely closer, hidden
in grainy dusk just out of view
beyond the high rim of the aerie,
toward which I have a sudden urge
to climb, limb by pagoda-style limb,
higher and higher to reverse the decades,
and peer over its edge into my bedroom
window: Will the boy be awake or asleep?
If awake, will I see him levitate as he so
often felt he did while falling asleep?
Will he suddenly remember to set
the wind-up copper alarm then groan
before relinquishing the quilt
at first pale sliver of daybreak
to deliver, house by house, the dark
news of a soaring Republic?

§

Now my family of eagles
are gone without a goodbye,
flown east for the winter
down a river tributary,
riding updrafts along bluffs
over on the Mississippi,
without leaving sign
(some talon marks)
that I'm welcome
to spend the night
at the top of their pine-
scented island
in the sky, suspended

high and safe
above the Republic's
highway noise, snug
under a loose
comforter of down
shed by chicks hatched
spring after spring.

§

Scavenger of mostly
dead gizzard shad churned up
by barge locks on the tamed Mississippi,
not so much feared as it is ignored
by the rest of the creature world: In full soar,
with wingspans long as the average
height of a man, their heads and tails
shimmer with glacial brightness
as dark-complected foreigners standing
beside me on the observation deck
of the National Eagle Center
duck whenever one glides low overhead.

§

Shinnying up the immense trunk
I grab for handholds in the bark's
furrows, catch my footing and breath
on the first thick limb, skeins
of light shining down
through the boughs, inked
and brushed by pine needles,
color of paper money, sheen
of fresh-minted coins
sifting down from slits
in the aerie's enormous weave,

as if overturning Dad's too dire
warnings that it doesn't grow
on trees or just fall from the sky—
though the serrated elm, lobed
oak and pointed maple leaves
that did as I wandered the autumn
woods sheaving them in wads
thicker than the dollar bills
I earned mowing and raking always
seemed the greater currency.

§

But Dad was tight and secretive
about money not wanting me
to know too much about how he made his,
rarely if ever taking me to visit
his classroom (I think I saw it once)
fearing I might follow into the low
pay option that misplaced
his talents and draconian
work ethic: So now I'm mowing
and raking my way back through
the years, shoveling waist-deep
snow from driveways, hauling
and stacking rows of cordwood,
while boyhood pals wait for me
to play capture the flag; yet I'm
washing and waxing, I'm learning
the value of a buck, sweeping
the basement, garage, driveway
and dog kennel, Dad's motto
A willing working is a happy worker
writ in his flawless penmanship

on my chore list still taped
to the fridge as I pull myself up
another limb closer to the aerie,
further up the family tree
from which I hear distant cries
of poor farmers with too many
kids to feed as Depression-era fears
pass down-limb into my father, still
girdling my dreams long after I'm born.

§

Nowadays
The fearsome eagle sings
Of markets
And material bling
I sing on my way up,
in poor imitation, my sought-
after voice of honey,
whiskey and blood,
only a growl in desperate
need of hair of the dog,
a shave and hot bath—
though at one point
I pretend I'm a young
Dakota brave
sneaking up
on a cliffside aerie,
unafraid of talons,
their sudden grasp that
could crush my wrist bones
as he plucks a single
long tail-feather
I'm wearing into my first

raid, my first bison hunt
shouting *Hoka-hey!*
Hoka-hey! Hoka-hey!
until I'm keening
the cries of an eagle as if
pissed off at the Republic
on behalf of all
eagles, everywhere.

§

But mostly I'm happy to use
the never-lost skills of a boy
who loved to climb the tree-tops,
hang monkey-like from vines
of the jungle-gym, son of Tarzan,
an ape-man swinging myself
with habile hand and opposable
thumb from limb to limb higher
toward the aerie, pulling myself
up into the primordial mists
of my boyhood, through the early-
morning shadows and moonlit
nostalgia of my paper route,
slow roseate bleeds of dawn,
through its rains and snows
now falling softly and softly
falling from the aerie's crude
yet intricate weave of sticks,
stronghold grown so large
a man might curl inside
for a night's reprieve
from the blood-
soaked headlines ripping

from sea to shining sea
the fabric of our Republic
like a thin worn sheet.

§

Under a tidal drift of stars,
without a book to read myself
asleep, I draw
a mighty eagle, star-
to-star my fingertips slowly
searching the path, connecting
each bright cosmic body
into a new unnamed constellation—
but even then, after Mom
takes the dipper and pours
warm cascades of bathwater I never
want to end down
my neck, even
after she tickles
my back with the lightest
of touches, and tucks
me in, I'm still
not sleepy; I need
a story I can take
back to my children:
myth of the aerie,
aerie without end,
high and safe,
as they drift toward sleep.

Water Lily Mischief in the Key of F

As children it was a big deal to pick a water lily
because they were protected and we feared
we'd shame ourselves by breaking a law,
even though no one would ever know.
Now we leave each one alone, gazing
at them as if they were all the beautiful
married women we've known, as we should
despite our inscrutable lust to do otherwise,
each beguiling flower a reminder
of how lustrous these women looked
on their wedding days an hour before
walking the aisle as if conjured
by libidinous gods in a church's anteroom
mirror, where in bras and panties as breathtakingly white
as water lilies, their skin as sun-warmed and silken
as summer lake water, five sirens caress wavering tendrils
of the goddess' hair. Drifting by thousands that are not
waiting for my hand to reach down from a green
canoe, I often think it wouldn't hurt to pick
just one, but which one would I choose? I'm too
humored by the stamen that's already
erect as every married nipple I've ever imagined
hardening in the outlet of my mouth. I'm
too mindful that a water lily opens its moist,
supple art at dawn, widest in noon light,
then closes it tightly by dusk, quite
the opposite of how we are when we sleep.
But with all of them dreaming wide open now

in bright August sunlight, I'm the only
lover whose slow glide across the water,
who with every slow dip and pull of the paddle
can send out ripples that pleasure so many,
so deeply under the sleep of no one's lids.

Lord's Prayer of Horses

Last night all our horses, thousands
upon thousands of horses, arrived
at once under the cover of darkness,
a great miracle of horses that woke me
(the light switch of every farmhouse
thrown on and suddenly lit) with a tidal
stampede of hooves, wave after wave
rushing in from uncut forests to the east,
horses fording rivers so thickly the water
damned and flooded out behind them,
patient horses that walked sure-footed down
switchbacks of the Rockies, streaming
pageants of dust across the Great Plains
that hang in the distance like plumes of rain;
tributary horses streaming up from plantations,
and down from the great windy steppes
of Alberta and Saskatchewan, a thunderous
migration of horses lured here, across oceans
of time from Arabia and Barbary,
Sorraia of the harsh Portuguese plains,
ghost horses of the long-extinct Tarpans
that ranged across the steppes of Ukraine;
horses arrived from Mexico via conquistador
ships sailing from Spain, from Andalusia;
a slow, epic flood of draft horses,
Belgians, Clydesdales, and Percherons
spilling out into floodplain fairgrounds,
felling swaths of river valley timber
as they plodded toward Amish farms
pulling wagonloads of fresh-cut firewood,

hungry for the strain of yokes and the easy
weight of the plow; Tyrolean Haflingers
eager to hitch up to their funereal buggies
and pull them with joyous clopping;
Appaloosas approaching with all four
hooves airborne at once, their flying
gallop descended from the fire-steeds
of the Nez Perce, on which Chief Joseph
and his heartsick tribe out-rode the U.S.
Cavalry for months: over 1,500 miles
of cunning, strategic jockeying that ended
like a racehorse whose lungs burst, coughing
blood just forty miles short of the finish line;
unfinished Paints streaming in from far-flung
ranches and flea-bitten rodeo rings, flashing
by like patches of moonlight running in place
across the surface of ten thousand lakes; wild
mustangs lured down and away from the remote
Pryor Mountains by their dreams of richer
forage and sweeter grain, by our night air honeyed
with the allure of orchards and fresh-cut hay; herds
of homesick Quarter Horses that streamed back
in reverse of their westward pioneer journeys
through time, loping across the high arid
Great Plains to arrive at dawn's first light
in love with the lissome female shapes
of our Midwestern hills, atop which they exalt
their riderless forms against the morning's
dusk, yearn for halter and saddle with steam
rising from their dark coats, their lather
of sweat giving off a pungent spice; where,
as they bow their heads grazing in reverence

135

to the remnant cadence of a vanished sea
of grass, small herds come running swift
as the wind, and greet us along fences,
to make this parceled earth consolable again.

Two Women

One the axe, the other heartwood

One the flower, the other its fuse

One a fountain, the other my thirst

One the spirit, the other flesh

One the body, the other blood

One the wound, the other its scar

One the hunt, the other the kill

One the chasm, the other the bridge

One the precipice, the other the leap

One the journey, the other my destiny

One the new snow, the other my tracks

One the moment, the other eternal

One the grace, the other my torment

One the music, rising and spherical,

The other an earthly, downward dance

Gators and Lesser Gods

§ advice left on my answering machine by Sappho Weingarten

Never buy a car that prates
instructions like a Zen parrot or stuff
yourself with a pizza before sex—fresh
blueberries are probably best. When gray
squirrels horde walnuts inside the bocce
court of your attic's plaster walls, don't
avoid the killing that must be done; same for mud
wasps nesting under porch steps. When your mind
weeds grow back from the self
doubt a hard-ass father planted in your gut, go find
a psychotherapist who can help you pull them
out by their roots; if she tolerates
your rants against country-club Republicans
and moonlights as a coloratura whose
voice makes God weep, as well as a gourmand
who whips up *Reine de Saba*
avec Glaçage au Chocolat with her eyes
closed, ask her to marry. If later
you find she turns a deaf
ear to your blind yelling
up winding flights of a tumbledown
Victorian perched on a hillbilly slant
whenever you lose your keys or wallet, rest
assured you'll grow older and happier
together in the comfort of a parlor
window air conditioner unit droning
away the stifling heat. If you've still got
a roving eye, trace this mantra nine
times into the steam on your bathroom

mirror upon waking: *I don't*
do affairs or divorce to avoid what'll only
bring a plague upon your house. My dear *Deus*
Ex Machina, love is hard
enough but so much harder when
trying to hoe two rows at once. Turning sixty,
you ought to shitcan poetry to run a country
filling station. Ah Friend, let's just hightail it
to that one untrammeled
sanctuary in Florida where we can stroll
among drowsing gators and wood storks stretched
out in full soar over a cypress swamp's
sweet musk, inhaling enough chthonian
irony to deflate a fleet of Goodyear blimps.

For the Love of Horses and a Woman

In my poem of great love,
I can no longer meet the gaze of horses
or part my lips over the skin of an apple.

Dead love old love first love new love
are all the sounds the wind makes
grazing the surface of the lake,
loping this canopy of northern forest.

At the ocean last summer waves pounded
like herd after herd of wild horses,
flying manes and thunderous roar of hooves
rushing toward my poem of great love.

When one leaf on a single hillside aspen
trembles amid the stillness of the forest,
I walk back to the cabin, start a fire,
brush, saddle, and ride my poem of great love.

Far from my land of horses and orchards,
I'm startled awake by an opera of wolves,
tumult of cemeteries and first blind thud
on your coffin in my poem of great love.

In the morning a raven sailing past
the kitchen window is only a raven,
but also a reminder how we die
only three times more slowly than our horses
and that every orchard will outlive us.

I've wandered the forest for days as if all
the wind's been knocked out of me,
desperate for sign of a trail that leads back
to our lost domain of horses and orchards,
a secret clearing with two horses saddled
in the orchard of my poem of great love.

The pathway of the moonrise glinting
across the lake follows me like my memory
of you riding barelegged, phlox and the sweat
of horses mixed with the scent of an orchard.

There's an ache of a wound like a nail
from the dock probing my bare foot
that I'll never be able to cook for you
except in my poem of great love.

Menstrual Love

Well after check
out time, deep
into their affair,
the fugitive
lovers are fucking
on a four poster
in a posh hotel:
She's on top
when her hand
moves to prop
another pillow
under his head,
leaving a perfect
handprint
of blood, whorled
lines he eyes
with amazement,
while kissing
the coppery
decoupage
across her chest
and neck; and later,
as they shower,
mesmerized
by the volume
of watery blood
flowing from
his inner thighs,
by her pose
of pained serenity,

as hot spray
thrums her back,
an image arises
of arrows piercing
San Sebastian's
female torso,
along with the spear
thrust and churned
into Christ's side,
and finally of a rag
soaked in vinegar
stuffed
into each other's
thirsting mouths.
While she strips
the bloodied sheets,
he slides bloody
cases off pillows,
and together
they hurriedly roll
these with a ream
of sanguinary white
towels they used
to wipe themselves,
into a big ball
outside the bathroom
door; a mound
he eyes warily
carrying
their suitcases
past as though
a dead child might
be wrapped inside.

Parable of the Nifty Guy at Loose Ends

Once before the bright high
noon reckoning of his life,
with a posse of money and marriage
worries hard on his trail through
the heat and dust of his boom-
to-bust thirty-seventh summer,
a rattlesnake bite

and venom of infidelity working
through his blood; a tourniquet
stanching his lust for another
man's wife; his repossessed
pseudo-horse on empty and too
far down a washboard road
to turn back, he guns it for a hideout

in the bluffs—saloon with a juke
box and farmgirl strippers, some trout
stream running outside—where the halter-
topped madam slides a triple
shot of rotgut along the worn
bartop he gulps in one throat-
burning swallow. When his vision
clears, he catches his own smirk

on the *Wanted: Dead or Alive*, dashing
in sepia—though there's nowhere
else but home or further back
into the hills. Squinting into the smoke-
stained back-bar mirror, he orders another

suddenly amazed he's among Social
Security drunks and pull-tab gamblers

who'll ride their chairs for hours. Even
as a voice calling out his name warns
the place's surrounded, orders him to toss
his pride through swinging doors, then ease
out slowly, hands raised high, the vigilante
bounty-hunting itchy trigger finger
of his conscience saying, *Vengeance
is mine*; I'm eager to repay
with a groin full of lead.

Hornets

All that not long-ago summer
I took it as my poetic duty
to dwell in Love and Beauty
while performing the most
menial tasks: whenever
I mowed or scraped
my peeling house, I summoned
her face and was gripped
by a trance as tightly
as my hands
clutched the hedge
trimmer—its blades
whirring at the *arbor*
vitae shredded a hidden
nest of hornets that
swarmed my bare
sweaty back flinging
me to the grass
with a seizure
of blessed stings.

Picasso's Last Moments at Mougins

Finally
all the lovers
whirl with neo-
tropical color, light as song
birds caught in a funnel
cloud that touches
down with the terrible
ear-to-rail howling
of a runaway freight,
lovers the mind
picks up running
as a twister sometimes
carries old jars, even
dairy cows or more
rarely a child
acres over the wheat
setting each one
down in the wind-
tormented grass as if
they only dreamed
this, unharmed.

Making Do

runnels
of March snow
stream from the roof

as if some indefinable
longing could seep
from the snowbanks
onto the street
gather into rivulets
that sheet toward the curb
course down the gutter
rushing into the storm sewer
grate that feeds a small
gurgling creek

whose current I can hear
roaring between its banks
deep and swollen
brown with runoff

until dusk
when it finally subsides
and snowmelt
slows to only a trickle
of loneliness tapping
the downspout

and I'm pleased
by puffs of geyser
steam from the grill

as Rose our yellow Lab
springs and pounces
like a brush wolf
after chipmunks
in a transplanted patch
of native bluestem

by the murmur
of a brook
from my neighbor's
heated birdbath
while an ocean

surf lilts from a six
lane freeway
over its barrier wall
as if muffled by dunes
along a warm beach

I might walk down to
if our little backyard
sledding knoll
weren't so scabbed
with snow and ice

under the first stars
sowing their light
like seed being
scattered and tossed
with generous handfuls
flung toward earth

Night on the National Mall

The only sound's a bleared
stream of headlights
like running
water I almost can't hear moving
in and out of earshot
across an immense
span of lawn between the Capitol
dome and a towering
spike ringed by fifty limp flags—
no sound downwind
of that limp circle except
an underwater hush
now magnified by the weight
of acres of darkening marble,
as if dusk's sealing me inside
the feeling of a tomb.

§

Shade trees pool
their shadows too deep, brimming
with threats of imagined danger
where lamps have burned out
along the gravel
walkway, the crunch
and release underfoot loud
as gnawing insects.

§

Powdery phalanx of Japan's
gift of the cherry trees
along the pewter-tinted
waters of the tidal basin,
now deserted as I drift
through the festival's
pastel-scented blossoms,
each cluster delicate, soft
as the skin of newborn's wrist—
moving away from Jefferson—tall,
aristocratic on his pedestal,
lips pressed too tight,
stance a little too
jaunty, his face perhaps
a touch smug as he
stares in perpetuity
across the once-fecund pools,
his shrine lit from within
like the eye of a giant
national security camera.

§

Earlier, by turns, everyone shooting
photos rapid as machine-
gun fire of the same thing:
war memorials, one's
polished granite
etched scrolls itemizing
names of the dead, while
another tries to capture the posture
of an uncle who was shot and bled
flag-red; his perfect bronzed
combat boots, fellow soldiers

in perpetual march, with boot-
falls that never touch down
suspended in mid-stride, mocked
by a paver's intermittent
crawl of ants.

§

Still, I might walk toward an eternal
flame, cross a bridge into lush
rolling green hills planted with flawless
white crosses; witness the painstaking
ritual and stoicism of tight-
jawed sentinels changing guard; and
later, kneel as inside a temple,
drawn by the moonlit glow
of Lincoln's cragged and warty
face, left hand curled at the knuckles,
his right upturned in a gesture
of national supplication,
melancholy eyes transfixed
by the soft webbed skid of a pair
of mallards landing in unison
on placid night waters, silent
rippling slivers of current, peace
that passes all understanding forever
trailing, closing in their wakes.

In the Valley of the Present

It's abundantly flagrantly clear
there's far too much grim
dire reality afoot in the world,
yet that's really nothing very new
under our benevolent morning
star ever since jealous Cain rose up
and slew his only brother Abel;
corrupt moneychangers seized
control of boy Jesus' temple;
bubonic plague decimated vast
sons and daughters of Europe;
howitzers of Manifest Destiny
exterminated our defiant Indians;
Nazis herded their sheep-slaves
into gas chambers at Auschwitz.

Yet in the valley of the present
shadow I shall not despair.
A long winter is passed:
lilac, tulip, bluebell, plum
thicket and apple orchard,
in full yet nascent bloom,
warblers in peak migration;
and waking from the next
ten or more sleeps my eye
will overflow with seeing,
my ear brim with hearing,
wildflower-scents abound
and every bone that's tired
or fearful of life or death

on earth, heavy with ruinous
word of its moment-by-moment
onslaught of disease, loss,
misfortune and chaos, will
instead hum with vital energy.

Fair Weather Cumulus

Before our imaginations shrank
to an idea of monotheism,
the gods made acrobatic
love and warred with clubs,
danced, feasted, and got drunk,
lusted and committed adultery
in stolen chariots, sometimes
tumbling blissfully unaware
with a bruised thud to earth
from cloud mattresses
of fair-weather cumulous.
§
How strange to be descended
from people who disabused
the Dakota of their mystic
belief in thunder beings
yet kept straight dour faces
as they explained angels, a virgin
birth and full bodily resurrection
then slaughtered their under-
studies along with vast bison
herds stampeding high undulant
plains faster than windswept
shadows of fair-weather cumulus.
§
With all earth's mammals, birds,
and fish still officially kicked
out of the Kingdom of Heaven,
our lonely widower God, denied
even the companionship of a pet,

must grow infinitely lonelier
as He wanders his barren
meadows and fauna-less foothills,
jabbing a crooked staff into plush
crags of fair-weather cumulus.

Autobiography

Blue flag iris bloom

In the lake mirror neither

Water nor flower

Fears

The soles of my feet are afraid of thistles.

My mind is afraid of itself.

My buttocks are sometimes afraid of the toilet in Florida

because I have read of a crocodile that emerged upwards from the
sewer.

My shin is afraid of bruising itself on the coffee table.

My left palm is afraid of its blister ripping open on the shovel's
wooden handle.

My palms flinch at the sight of the square nails spilled

onto the floor near the feet of Velasquez's self-absorbed Christ.

The flesh in my side is afraid of the spear in the museum of Roman
art.

My luck is afraid of running out at the wrong time.

My soul is afraid of walking under water towers.

My liver is afraid of bourbon.

My penis is afraid of northern pike slashing for bait.

I am afraid of the drowned boy's eyes staring up

as I walk the path around the lake.

It is the beginning of fear when I see carpenter ants in the kitchen.

I am nearly afraid my bird dog may die of a tick-borne disease.

I am afraid as I rub her fur to find them swelled and shiny,

the size and texture and weight of wild grapes.

The nape of my neck is afraid of the swoop of bird shadows.

I am deeply afraid of falling asleep with my hands folded softly
together over my navel the way the dusty hands of corpses are
clasped in eternal repose.

I am afraid to die tomorrow or the next day or the day after that.

I am only slightly less afraid to die within a fortnight.

I am afraid of the moment that I become aware I am eating moldy
bread.

I am afraid of peering over the wall of the cistern.

I am still afraid of Caesar Vallejo's prediction that he will die in Paris on a rainy day.

I am afraid that our worst actions will be without consequences in an afterlife.

In the alley I am always afraid to open the lid of the green dumpster.

On the trail through a rich bottomland forest my shins are naturally afraid of brushing against the serrated edges of stinging nettles.

The lining of my anaphylactic throat grows afraid as I peel and eat a plate of Gulf shrimp.

In quiet desperation I fear late November through the winter solstice.

I am afraid of all mealy textures but especially of stale cornbread.

My carotid artery is afraid of box-cutters.

My solar plexus is afraid of airplane turbulence.

My body's core temperature is afraid of capsizing on Lake Superior.

I am afraid that I will always suffer from a permanent lack of wit.

My scalp itches in fear of a child's head lice, especially their nits.

I am afraid of not having more and more years to spend in vain.

My future grows afraid of the remembrance of the image of Reagan waving goodbye with a half-shaven head.

Lice

Soles of my feet afraid of thistles, my mind
afraid of itself. My ass sometimes
afraid of Florida toilets because I
read of a croc that rose from a sewer. My shin
always afraid of bruising itself; my blister
of ripping open on the spade's wooden handle. My palms
flinch at the sight of square nails spilled
near the feet of Velasquez's self-absorbed Christ. Flesh
in my side afraid of the spear in a gallery of Roman art.
My luck afraid of running out. My
soul afraid of walking under water towers. My liver
afraid of bourbon. My skinny-dipping
balls afraid of northern pike slashing for bait. I'm
desperately afraid of the drowned boy's
eyes staring up as I hike around the lake. Fear
kicks in when I catch the conga-
march of carpenter ants in the kitchen. Nearly
convinced my bird dog may die of a tick-borne
disease as I comb her
fur to find them latched, swollen
and shiny as wild grapes; the nape
of my neck afraid of the swoop of bird shadows;
the child inside me still afraid to peer
over the wall of the bottomless
cistern. How long will I live
in fear of Caesar
Vallejo's prediction he'll die in Paris
on a rainy day; that my worst actions will be without
consequences in an afterlife? Will the lining of my allergic
throat always tighten and itch at the sight of raw shrimp? In the back

alley I'm afraid to open the lid of the green dumpster.
My carotid artery's afraid of box-cutters; solar-plexus
of airplane turbulence; body's core
temperature afraid of capsizing on Lake Superior. My scalp
itches in fear of a child's head lice; my future
grows afraid of the remembrance of a narcoleptic
president waving goodbye from my hometown with a half-shaven
    head.

Internet Porn

Jonah—more
and more enamored
with subtle
variations, peculiar
hues, unusual,
intriguing petal-shaped
fins of every
fish in the sea—drifted
further out until
until he couldn't see
ashore, yet no longer
caring about any real
fishing, didn't
notice a shadow
circling his dinghy
until it suddenly rose,
swelled enormously
and swallowed his
whole being
gone limp.

Invitation to My Opening

for my next project
an installation at the Walker

curated by a full color
cardboard cut-out

of the honorable Mister
George Whipple

only the finest tissue
Charmin Extra

Soft in order to begin creatively
inhabiting the crevasse

of my bunghole for thirty-three straight
single wipe days

somewhat like found art
on each plait framed

in an odor proof
plexiglass case

as if hovering
over an imaginary

wildflower meadow
patterns rise

natural as the dust
on butterfly wings

a whole wall
of shit taking flight

June

Monotony sprouts its rows of tendril
green wisps that shine with solstice
heat from damp rain-
blackened cornfields—only
beautiful just before
they flourish—now suddenly too
lush and drooping with the dull
tired weight of their fronds.

Passed over, sad, fading and neglected,
flowers still displayed in nurseries
wait with orphaned faces, the last
likely never to be chosen.

In meadows and forests, expectant
mothers grow serene in burrows,
drowse in thickets while restless
fathers wander stricken
with an aimless diligence.

Beyond each forest-meadow
edge, without warning, foliage
obliterates all the forest's sight-lines—
a desperate moment for hikers
trapped beneath a canopy's
fallout of infinite
shadow—sinister with waist high
nettles, strangler vines, avian
shrieks hidden within
an apocalypse of dense
suffocating green.

Self-Pity in the Midwest

Lives in a boomtown but dotes on hardscrabble hill country

Happily married yet still spellbound by all the pretty ones

Has two healthy children but all the neighbors have one more

Trains a champion Labrador retriever disappointed it won't point

Paddles a cedar-strip canvas canoe yet covets a teakwood sailboat

Wanders Driftless backroads longing to be nomadic in Montana

Tends an expansive kitchen garden yet wants an entire farm

Fly fishing beneath picturesque bluffs pines for snowcapped Rockies

Out drinking with old friends wishing for new more literary ones

Could easily drive to Minneapolis yet insists on dining in Chicago

Crisscrosses the Great Plains imagining the Serengeti

Hunts trophy whitetails bored they're not bugling elk

Studies native prairie remnants regretting lost seas of grass

As coyotes yip and yodel yearns for a timber wolf's howl

Earns a master's degree but craves a doctorate's prestige

Practices morning tai chi lamenting it's not afternoon zazen

Raised a free-spirited gnostic yet marries into Catholic guilt

Fall Again

Fields of goldenrod have burned out

while the last
grasshoppers spring
stiffly or not at all, armored
bodies weighted by this first
hard frost, brittle
filaments of Indian
grass ablaze, the reservoir
gelatinous and freezing to a cataract
of clear black. From this old

wooden footbridge, I fear
for the future
of water-striders propelling
the immensity of their shadows
across an almost-still creek pool.
As a generation of leaves sinks
in slow-motion whirl, pasting
their exhausted forms
to streambed cobble, the whole

world's dying
without effort as another
fit of rain and wind rips
its color from the trees—a little
more each day as fall reveals
winter's secret I have no
words for: other
than it is our lives.

Patents

My newest registered patent for a dog
seatbelt, so Rose can ride shotgun, nose
pressed to the dashboard vents
sniffing the lush
fetor of hog barns, stubble fields dotted
with Canada geese, the oily
black rags of crows flapping past,
scampering killdeer and car-flattened
raccoon arriving in the damp
cool air without my fear
of a life-ending accident. I don't
ever want to lift her
limp body, fox-red fur flecked
with glass and leaking blood
into a tallgrass wildflower ditch
like ones she loves to hunt. So I borrowed
an Amish friend's cracked
leather horse harness
designing adaptations no one had ever
dreamed before. Outdoor retail giant
Cabela's also intends to distribute a dog
toilet modified from a stolen Mayo
Clinic bedpan that flushes with a single
bark, canine or otherwise for owners
too impatient to teach their very best
friend the flush-woof. I cribbed the voice-
activated inflections from a cultish
baby's board book, *Doggies* by Boynton, further
evidence of my inventive genius. Once
after I zapped a younger, higher-strung

Rose, yelping, high into the air
for chasing an estrus-crazed doe
with repeated taps on my shock
collar controller turned all the way up
as she sauntered back into range, I pinned
her down by the shag of her neck, forcing
her foamy mouth into the forest
loam. With her fecund
eyes and grave muzzle, Rose insisted that I
consider strapping one
around my own
neck modifying its electronics
so it shocks me to Kingdom
Come each time I yell
Fuck! after she flushes
and I miss a grouse
or pheasant.

Leaving Deer Camp

Long past growing season,
Several weeks after first frost,
A late spell of unseasonable warmth pushes up
A cluster of dandelions through gravel
At the entrance of the long driveway,
Buttery and golden in full bloom—

Like the stubborn part of me that never wants to leave,
That never wants anything to end,
Flowering just as things are suddenly over,
Always the last one willing to depart,
The forest bare, grey, solemn, waiting for snow.

My companions already crossed over,
Thrust back into their everyday
Lives of jobs, debts, wives and children.

Reluctantly, stretching the heavy chain across
The gravel drive, I drop the hook, closing myself off
On the other side of deer camp, like a prisoner
Staring from beyond the gate, not wanting
To turn away, cleaving myself
From this last November flourish.

for Samuel Butterfass

Girl at the Strip Mall

There was nothing special
about the day. After work.
Coldest hour of November.
Just after dusk. Walking
down to the *Miracle Mile*.
In cold drizzle. Intent
on a bottle of red.
Except for this girl. Really
a young woman. Maybe less
than half his age. Sobbing
along a pillar of the strip
mall. Protesters all gone
home for the day. Torn
windbreaker. One arm
bandaged to hold its
stuffing in. Both nostrils
crusted with blood. Split
lip. Cliché of streaked
mascara. As she weeps.
He doesn't stare. Yet
can't help glancing
back after he passes
her by. Once. Twice.
Except his pace
slows. To a shuffle.
As he hears himself,
his own gentle voice
in his mind asking
with heartfelt
lovingkindness,

if she needs help.
Some money? A cab
ride somewhere? Is there
someone I can call for you?
His legs now anchored
by a weight he can not
pull free from. He feigns
interest in a vacant store
front's coat hangers, empty
display tables, metal shelving.
Studying her reflection
in the plate-glass. Yet
not long. Her face
puttied by makeup.
Black lipstick now
dangling a cigarette,
her hands shaking too
uncontrollably to light.
An invisible undertow
already grabbing ahold
of his ankles. At first
subtle but now
carrying him away
with a surge of resolve
in the opposite direction.
Until its momentum stalls
in the gleam of liquor
through the store's thick
glass door. With its string
of bells that will jingle
when he pushes it open.
Except he waits. Solemn

under hooded sweatshirt.
Until she walks briskly past.
A whiff of perfume.
Further and smaller
down the sidewalk.
Out of his life forever.

Nametag *Peggy*

Where she came from
You'll never know
Other than it was a hard
Long road to the back

Of the convenience
Store service counter
Where she always
Greets you smiling

Sincere and bug-eyed
Lids shadowed turquoise
Thick as a child's mashed
Streaks of sidewalk chalk

Her voice like gravel
Scraping bottom
Of a whiskey barrel
Hello Dear

How are you today
Through neon lipstick
And stained mouthful
Of capped teeth

As you give something
Like alms for a cup
Of stale coffee
Or lottery ticket

For the chance
To conjure her former
Life as a gypsy
Fortune teller

Bead artist
Crash pad
Hippie strung out
At Haight-Ashbury

Someone lured me
To a gal out there
With mist in her eyes
And blossoms in her hair

Oversized lavender daisy
Hairclip still blooming
From her wild frizzed
Cascade of greyed

Locks dyed half pink
Like Janis' if she'd kicked
Smack to ramble
On as long as Peggy

Whose identical tattoo
A Florentine bracelet
That waif personally
Drew out on her wrist

Backstage at Monterey
After tripping together
Slow-kissing in between
Swigs of Southern Comfort

Swaying front & center
In bell bottoms onstage
With Grace Slick at muddy
Peace-soaked Woodstock

Areolas rippling through
A loose white blouse entranced
By Altamont's strange dream
Killing vibe of wickedness

First aboard the last hurrah
Of Festival Express' non
Stop jam sessions & all
Night partying with Jerry

Garcia's cock in her ass
A special kind of fame
Rivaled only by her best
Friend the Butter Queen

Stratospheric names
The Internet drops
Like acid on the tip
Of her tongue's

Photographic
Memory of sucking
Her generation's
Pantheon of genius

Dionysian energy
Of their minds
That launched her
Into rarefied orbit

Paramour goddess
Groupie girlfriend
Unpaid porn star
Nihilistic muse

Nectarine, nectarine
Reflection living in a dream
I'll win her love
She'll be my queen

Hearing the first riffs
Holding the notebook's
Lyrics she inspired
Played on the radio

Decades after
The party ended
With too many shared
Needles and friends

Dead by overdose
By suicide her own
Womb suffocated
By a growing

Family of abortions
Save for the last
Girl she refused
To kill and carried

Father unknown
From a cheap motel
Into an anonymous
Penniless gut

Wrenching adoption
That fed her
Tramped out
Chain smoking

Soul to a summer
Fair circuit's band
Of misfit carnies
Tilt-a-Whirl's

Kaleidoscopic
Midway hustle
For a decade
Long angry fix

In depraved
Trailer camp
Orgies with midgets
Writhing squished

To grotesque fatness
In the hermaphrodite's
Sick joke of fun
House mirrors

That shattered
Into a million
Jagged shards
Cutting inside her

As she stared
Into an apparition
Of pure innocence
Laughing aboard

The miniature
Choo-choo
That transfigured
Into a graffitied

Boxcar trundling
Her down the rails
To nowhere in rat
Piss shaking DTs

Strike out on your own
Destiny unknown
Like a rolling bone
Without compass home

But for an uncanny
Notion she'd find her
Someday somewhere
Transfixed

By the face of an angel
As long as she kept
That blind faith
Walking the line

With her collar
Turned up
To a cold mean
Lonely wind blowing

Through all the nights
Since her rebirth
Somehow spared
AIDS grim specter

Like a curse lifted
Blessing her anonymous
Second life finding
Solace in ordinary

Steady work
As shift manager
Sometimes surprised
By her own grand

Motherly face
In the breakroom
Mirror stuck in this
Northern Podunk

She doesn't love
Or hate when
Its rivers freeze
And summer ends

With a first snowflake
Storm through her
Trailer court window
As she sifts through

Unpublished Polaroids
Jim's buried in Paris
Mick still a fountain
Of leaping youth

Robert silent yet Jimmy
Facetimes once a year
Hey Merry Christmas
Fingering new chords

That always inspire
Just enough courage
To retry a tentative
Hand at writing

Her memoirs
By candlelight
Meteor showers
Outside her trailer

Flesh of stardust
I am golden carbon
And I've finally made my way
Back to the garden

Where she tends
A self-tilled patch
With hummingbirds
Buzzing her hibiscus

Vultures

They soar without effort
buoyant and tottering
on dihedral wings, kettle
lazily adrift on an afternoon's
rising thermals, as if magnetized
to every moment of the wind
pleasuring their feathers.

They glide in loose
haphazard gyres of pure
enchantment slowly
massaging the shapes of the bluffs—
as if by powers of absolute detachment
or insouciance—nonchalantly coaxing
death out of the valley,
from the slopes of secret ridges
and dark, bosky ravines.

Perched on a ribcage—
benevolent, violently
taking turns—a shrouded
cloister of bald pink heads
rips and probes
hollows of the rain-
dilapidated pelt, plunging hooked
beaks into the stinking carcass. One gobbles
the clouded succulence of an eyeball.

The fur ripples,
the chest cavity rises and falls

as if it's still breathing—
undulant the motions of maggots,
a rapid free association of dream
images riffling inside a putrid
deer's permanent sleep—

such grotesqueries
they greedily erase from fields
and ditches, in exchange
for the pleasure of soaring
in endless dihedral drift.

Ode to Walter Mitty

It's finally impossible,
despite my once malignant
tumor of envy, to keep on wanting
to be someone else—such dreams
mercury thin as the sound
of *Blonde on Blonde* except
if you're born on an Iron Range
where the snow and wind hits
heavy on the borderline, Bobby
Zimmerman forever dying,
thrown from a motorcycle
into the rebirth of his cigarette
charred voice, suddenly
transfigured one day at a time, lyric

by lyric—finally impossible to stay
the fool who wishes to be someone
else, even as much as I still want
to be Deano at the peak of his eternal
essence of cool, crooning with Frank
and Sammy in '61 at the Sands,
Marilyn in a tight
glitter of sequins draped
on one arm, raised highball
gleaming in the other. I grew up

chewing tobacco, on cheap
beer driving township gravel
through cornfields, convinced I'd be
Shakespeare-brilliant and immortal

all the way through that
preeminent belle époque
that eluded my thirties, my forties, such far-
fetched notions finally fading

like everyone's name
erased beyond recognition
on the lichen-splotched stones
of a lost pioneer cemetery I wandered
into, most toppled like tablets
under their own weight, stories
that will never be unsealed, their last
chiseled words decaying into forest.

Beyond the Widening Pale

I have always relished being
a creature that can march a passage
of Shakespeare through his head
while my legs are sucked
downward into the mute
chthonian odor and ooze
of a duck marsh. Meanwhile

the stores go on selling
consumers go on buying
commuters go on driving
marketers go on presenting
churchgoers go on worshipping
as if all is always momentarily
right with the world. Except

just before dusk, as a stubble
field's dark bovine shapes
meld into one docile
beast drifting toward a barn
while an invisible mist
net fastens silence tight
to the enormous crown
of a river cottonwood. Until

sheared by a last gunshot,
all autumn's migrating
blackbirds rush to escape,
lifting as one spiraling gyre
feeding itself as it spins
outward without end,
like thread sewing itself
into a pinhole of the void.

Alone Among Mermaids

Through ice and cold and snow
Into the tropical sanctum
Of their indoor
Archipelago, one
By one they arrive
Unbidden—until after many

Laps, after touching
And pushing off without pause
Without rest from the sheer
Underwater reef wall,
I'm surrounded, overtaken
By a dozen
And more leaping in, flutter
Kicking almost
Naked, aggressive,

Scattered, elliptical, delicate
Architecture of kneecaps,
Tender a shoulder blade,
Irresistible a birthmark,
Pattern of freckles on a thigh,
Cleft of buttocks and painted
Toes in swift glide
Thrusting in tandem so
Deeply focused, so far beyond
The casual solitudes, so
Deeply alone even one

Sharing my lane
Less than an arm's length
From caresses
Of my underwater imaginings—

Surely another glance
And I might perish
My flesh
Strewn among the rocks

Festival of San Sebastian: Old San Juan

for Paul Kemp & *John Olson*

Spilling from *bodegas,*
seething, knotting
and unknotting like happy
vipers thronging sidewalks,
spilling from *zaguanes*, tropical
stuccos, down the blue
grey cobblestone, *callejónes'*
slag-iron; sweaty
wandering drunk, manic
into the night straining its waist
against the Milky Way while
everything's still
possible in these hours that
won't end. Sandals
and sneakers thrum, bare
feet grip molded iron toward
the *Plaza de los Muertos*, drawn
by a band's basso
throb and strobing hip
hop beat that
massages the restless
ocean breeze. To dance oblivious

over the eardrums of the dead
into the pale daybreak in mockery
of the departed who want to shatter
the bones of their fists—to shout—
bashing their eyeless
socketed skulls to dust,

so desperate to pull these
young down, by their ankles,
by the veins in their wrists, centuries
of wave after chaotic wave
awakened and unable to
resist their urge to quell
the primal
deafness of youth; to endure
another minute their own
dusty wedding gowns and worm
eaten suits beneath
the plaza aroused without
release.

Mapping Aeries

I dream myself here
Before I arrive
From after death

From the ghost world
Where I am gliding
Toward my future

Guided into birth
Kept safe by the soar
And wingspan of eagles

Medicine eagles turning
Slow transparent circles
Sending down spirit-armor

The shape of my journey
The flow of air currents
Over the surface of earth

Migrations that push out
In every direction, random
Myriad and untraceable

Winding out & looping back
Over forests & river valleys
Coastlines & lakeshores

Riding updrafts buoyant
On afternoon thermals
Always mapping aeries

§

Searching as a child
The last aeries so rare
They almost cease to exist

For years not seeing an eagle
Surrogate hawks and falcons
Turning gyres wherever I go

Climbing to peer into nests
Songbirds drawing perfect
Circles, soft woven spheres

High & safe until my psyche
Thins like an eggshell
Made fragile by DDT

Our shared recovery
Arduous and slow
Climbing sheer cliffsides

Seeking on foot, by canoe
A young brave's single
Long eagle tail feather

Drawn north to Ojibwa country's
Tallest peak, Eagle Mountain
Seeking my vision at its summit

South into Dakota territory
Wandering without destination
Down the semi-frozen Mississippi

Nearing Wabasha waves
Of spirit eagles study me
At eye-level from the trees

§

Winter solstice eagles in vivid
Irruptions as in dream
Migrating south for open water

Downstream of Prairie Island
Nuclear power plant's release
Of gigantic thermal bubbles

February eagles in slow glide
Fishing swift churning rapids
Below lock and dam gates

Silhouettes of winter eagles
Like penguins on Lake Pepin's
Oracular ledge of shelf ice

Chief Wapasha's spirit eagles
Drawn by strong natural currents
Keeping the main channel ice-free

My guardian eagles lining
Riverbank cottonwoods
Draped in ancestral mystery

Always in flight over
The bluffs soaring in circles
That cut a hole through time

§

Mapping aeries in March
When eagles are mating, courting
In risky acrobatic aerial display

Walt Whitman's dalliance
Of eagles a rushing flourish
Of initial amorous contact

Clinching talons, cartwheeling
Each pair a living fierce gyrating
Wheel locked in fatal free-fall

Unclasping at the last moment
Returning to nests where each
Female stares like the Sphinx

Mapping aeries small and new
Decades-old weaves of sticks
Deep as hot-air balloon baskets

Invited by a single wedded pair
My family raising its young
Atop a reservoir's white pine

§

Lissome swoop of foraging eagles
Supple unfurled talons skimming
River surface clutching gizzard shad

Fat summer lilypond bass sinking
One's flight as she struggles to rise
With each prodigious wing flap

My parent eagles with panfish
Supper clamped talon to branch
Regurgitating down eaglet's throat

Years of Northwoods eagles over
Sky blue waters, heads and tails
Shimmering glacial brightness

Farm eagles perched atop a ribcage
Lording over road-killed whitetail
Always wary of my good intentions

Amish Country eagles gliding buggy-
Level leading me along gravel backroads
Feasting on offal of butchered Holsteins

Reclusive trout stream eagles
Scrutinizing my slow approach
Invisible on low-slung oak limbs

Leaping with phantom's whoosh
Humid wingbeats against my face
Rush of the breath of mapping aeries

§

Through my headstrong twenties
My urgent, worrisome thirties
My humbling focused forties

No longer seeking any reward
Beyond the shape of the journey
Of mapping aeries, old and new

Up and down islanded channels
Swamp and floodplain forests
Solitary backwaters, tributaries

Nine on branches of the Zumbro
Seven in Whitewater Valley
Two along Trout Run Creek

My life's work complete
Yet forever unfinished
Hike after hike I was led here

This morning on snowshoes
Through spindled hardwoods
Down the banks of a frozen river

My guardian eagle slumped
Where she had gone to sleep
Down in a grassy swale

Waiting with headdress feathers
Waiting in snowed-over grass
Dreaming us from the beginning

Abe Yoder

Such long days, black and white, no leaves or songbirds in this edging-ever-closer to an alpine timberline, January sun blinding off fresh snow, air almost too thin for breath. I still miss my wife in her wool shawl and navy head scarf at the clothesline framed by the sunporch window. Daughter-in-law Martha and her girls take Anna's place stacking freeze-dried denim shirts and trousers, one atop the other, then hang the laundry above the parlor stove to steam. Our young working daily alongside parents and siblings gives me hope that our ways—living in this world, but not being of it—might yet survive. Once, so much younger, I rode a gondola up Pikes Peak then hiked Barr Trail to a cirque overlook—that memory so vivid, a mirror image of the other invisible mountain I'm still climbing, though others can tag along only so far, edging closer to where the last trees thin out to dwarf shrubs, tiny gold and purple wildflowers, rivulets of snowmelt purling through alfalfa-green alpine tundra. Soon I'll weave my last throw rug passing my loom on to a beloved great-granddaughter. Long winter evenings, when my stamina's up, I join the others in the lantern-glow on a milk stool amid the familiar smells of hay and manure, and pungent coats of our Holsteins and draft horses. I don't know why being in a barn among dairy cows has always made me happiest. Though I can't help with chores, it's still good to be among children, even the youngest toting pails to the bulk tank. I'd like to live into another August for the fresh-cut oats drying in contoured rows, boys out driving the binders, sun-bonneted women and girls stacking the bundles, burnished oat shocks one last time, my buggy horse clopping along gravel, the sound of joy itself. No one plans to outlive friends and family but now nearly everyone I once knew and loved is gone. My time on earth's the slow drip of the kitchen tap, the trickle of glacial melt from the snowfield's edge. Even in high summer's intense sun, an alpine wind gusts sharp across my face, tactile with loss, the memory of Anna's hair when she let it down, after her bath damp and fresh as apple blossoms. Her warm shins somehow cool under a single summer sheet. Late winter of my life, I am keen to pass afternoons in my sunroom weaving or penning a letter to my last living cousin, walking to the mailbox giddy as I open it weeks later to find a reply. Community scribe these last fifty years, I always start my weekly entry for *Die Botschaft* with a bit of philosophy, such as *the supreme happiness of life is the conviction we are loved*, then follow this with news of farming; weather; family warmth and humor after *gamay*. Dismayed how I grew so old so quickly, I read in *Psalms* dozing off to glacial brightness glinting off fence-line snowdrifts— my favorite window scene. When I dream—often of late—it's an endless Great Plains view as I climb. Slow going, I often halt to catch my breath, while a procession of faces appears on the horizon drifting toward me from when I was a child—forgotten aunts, uncles, cousins, friends, neighbors, so many others from reunions, weddings, and funerals, most of whom I can't or only dimly remember when I'm fully awake. I startle awake just as the summit comes into view, certain I'll join everyone waiting, finally able to see God—not with my eyes—who clothes me in mercy, the light I'll wear in place of my body.

Field Notes in Late Winter

dormant
the wildflowers,
grasses, by stalk,
by stem in every tint
beige to russet,
by their brittle
spent seed-heads
shivering in wind;
twist one off
crush it
to release &
inhale its sweet
cured potpourri:
ah yes purple
prairie clover

leafless the trees,
shrubs, by shape
of trunk, branch
& canopy,
bark's hue
and texture,
by your hands
massaging thick
rough furrows,
others with tight
smooth skins:
shagbark
hickory feels
like the sound
of its name

high up,
or hidden, let
birds come by ear,
call and song,
whistle,
twitter,
chortle,
burble,
eyes wide shut
as if blind,
taking delight
in melodies
tumbling pure
and innate:
first bluebirds
wood thrushes
are back

True Believer/Small Miracle

I'm a true believer in spring,
great awakenings, little resurrections:
waxen tips of daffodils thrust up
through melting snow, impaling
last autumn's oak leaves; peepers
chorusing a marsh back to life;
a woodcock's aria tumbling back
to the apple orchard at first light.
As I hike toward my old
bird dog's hilltop grave,
where I buried her body wrapped in flannel
hunting shirts under a sentinel burr oak,
I half expect to be dumbfounded
by an empty tomb, yet arrive
relieved that coyotes haven't
dug Rose up, not disappointed
that the slight mound is settling.
Fresh grief wells up in the raw space
under my breastbone, yet my time
of weeping's over. Her protégé, Oshie,
stands quizzically astride the grave,
a cleft dug with spade and pickaxe
into rocky soil, friable layers
of Decorah shale—shards my wife
placed as a marker in shape of a paw,
the five old rough grass-stained pads
I used to rub—even this fossiliferous
life of the dead now placed
in the memory of the living,
the realm in which Rose ascends

daily, forever walking
a spirit trail beyond her life,
in and out of my field of vision,
here or there a few moments wading
a shallow creek pool as she hunts
fruitlessly for minnows, always with a curious
tilted muzzle. This morning she's loping stride
for stride with her young soulmate—
their reddish beige coats merge with
reddish beige grass—coursing
paths only visible as the rustle
and shiver of switchgrass,
unmistakable jangle of her tags
a small miracle on the spring wind.

Suite to Prairies

In the Ditch

A strip of native
grasses, forbs, wild
flowers in the ditch *shooting*
star rattlesnake master
prairie smoke bottle
gentians and somehow
nesting bobolinks and sedge
wrens who thrive nowhere
else find this last resilient
isthmus after weeks
migrating plowed black
seas sprouting endless
rows of soy and corn.

Dark Fields of the Republic

Acre upon acre of monocrop
green, so much green my eyes can't
absorb its greenness. Fronds
bow their heads as if they're
every mother who ever wept
over sons killed at war, all
weeping at once; young woman
weeping for love; girls weeping
over dogs and horses; old
women weeping beside
caskets as their husbands sleep
with clasped hands. Every
stalk swells with the juice
of grief and from the underside
of each frond something darker
than grief gathers and flows.

Funeral

The hearse waits at the white
frame church steps, where
a maple flames without
burning as more cold
embers fall to the grass.
The gravedigger cups
his hands around a match
then exhales into the pit, felt
green tarp over the fresh mound.
A north wind rushes through
like a cold dry river; my fatigued
bird dog's passed out
on a heated passenger seat
of heaven while no one—
not wife, not lover, not
mother, father, sister, brother,
not friends, not sons nor daughter—
on earth knows where I am.

The Killers

Out here we're at war
with the earth. Artillery
claws of combines, spoils
stored in monolith silos. At sunrise
invisible shooting begins, one
barrage then another. Then silence.
From the shadow of each
bunker, through broken windows,
over cattail sloughs and spruce
windbreaks, every
winged angel disguised
as a bird trying to flee, shot
on sight. At dusk, the killers
clamp a boot down on pairs
of outstretched wings,
and rip out their breasts.

Antlers

Bright red shell casings:
a skirmish. Not far off,
just inside the woods:
bloated with flies, stiff
loll of tongue, cataract
stare, head scalped
for its antlers.

Heroes

Madson and Hammerstrom,
dead. Now Gruchow,
by his own hand. Last
chief, Joe Medicine
Crow, dead at 102.
Who's left?
What's left? The horse
a museum piece
beyond barbwire. Nature
driven onto reservations—
prairies stripped, beaten
back to railroad
embankments, pioneer
cemeteries; creeks dozed
into straight lines,
ditched; potholes
drained, tiled, plowed
under. All my heroes
dead and gone.

Fumarole

Under the night-
grey skin of dawn
frost sparkles mauve
across a stunted
nondescript acre
of gravelly
weeds in back
of a convenience
store along Interstate 90,
where in the last
of the moonlight,
Rose squats,
steam rising
from this dark
fumarole—and for
a moment, I'm back
in Yellowstone, eyes
locked on this
small vent's faint
white puffs
though a crust
of travertine.

Beneath the Surface

Gunmetal dawn,
against the pale
ambient dirty leaf-
smoldering yellow
orb of prairie town,
steam, or smoke,
as from a basin,
rises windlessly
from chimneys,
pipes and vents,
as if magma's
hidden, flowing
everywhere just
beneath this flat
frozen earth.
Ahead, the mirage
of an ethanol plant
fumes geyser-like,
as if ready to blow.

Life Mirrors Art

Lavender dusk
with winter's first
snowflakes: a flurry
that swiftly gathers
momentum
until the scene
through my truck
windshield's so saturated
with falling snow
snow's falling
as if suspended,
dotting coal
black furrows
of plowed earth
like a pointillist
canvas so fresh
and luminous it will
never dry.

The Heartland

here in the heartland
on back roads way out
on the frozen prairie teens
discover entertainment
in drinking & driving gravel
roads late into the night
most often no one is killed
no mothers must grieve
as *Jack & Diane* graduate
find jobs marry have kids
who grow into bored teens
who discover the desolate
thrill of drinking while
driving gravel on winter
nights far on the prairie

Sumac Tea

For about thirty
seconds out walking
one bitter winter morning,
I grew immeasurably
certain that God as infinite
mercy reincarnates
the soul of every unborn
as a curled flower head
rising from
sumac thickets,
into these velvety
sprigs of dark
red berries.

(Sometimes you can break
one of your thoughts off
by its stem,
place it upside down
in a glass of cold water
that turns slowly amber,
then drink its mildly sweet
singularly delicious tea.)

All for Alex

In Grand Meadow, poetic
license for a Podunk
prairie town, at a benefit for the four
month old girl who needs a new
liver, it's a Friday night standing-room
only crowd inside Grumpy's
where even the girl's mom,
dancing in a welter of *All for Alex*
tees, is in high spirits. The bartender,
mixing my Beam & Sevens strong,
with only a splash of Seven, has
to shout over the rock band. Cigar
smoke makes my eyes water. Someone
says *forecast's for a foot
of snow*; someone else, *record yields but
prices're brutally low*. No one
asks what I do, and all the men
talk without irony, the way
they live, so fully
themselves, each with a right
arm crooked at the elbow, a drink
held over his heart.

Ordovician

I hike up an emerald
pasture's switchbacks cut
by cattle hooves into a hillside,
each narrow trail spilling
fossiliferous limestone,
small marine creatures once
the bottom of ancient shallow
seas far down at the equator:
I'm both here
and there, thousands
of miles away yet still
in the same place.

Hearts of Oak

All along this Iowa-
Minnesota border, the oldest
men have hearts of oak. In seed
caps and overalls, they wave
while opening rusty mail
boxes with a gnarled hand. Their limbs
strengthen and thicken, their roots
grown so far into the soil
they farmed they won't
relinquish the earth; the only
way they'll die: when a wind
storm such as last night's bends
and twists the canopies,
lunges and hurls
itself so violently into branches
and limbs that it rips
open a trunk's heartwood, shearing
them off at the strongest
place, exactly at chest height.

Sketches from a Hunter's Notebook

I walked an estimated ten
miles today while my yellow Lab, Rose,
whose natural pace is five times faster
than a man's, ran two marathons
through thickest possible cover—
cattail sloughs, bulrushes, reed
canary grass and razor-sharp cane—
her nose rubbed raw, an open wound,
hindquarters quivering
with muscle spasms as she passes
out beside me on the passenger seat.
I caress her brow like a feverish child's.
Not even the fetor of a McDonald's
rouses her as we idle at the drive-thru;
a girl's voice: May I take your order?
Really, five quarter-pounders, no buns?
No cheese or ketchup or anything?
On the interstate in the early
winter dark my hands tear greasy
pieces from the first hot patty
like a priest breaking apart the host,
placing each morsel on the tongue
of this enfeebled parishioner who
licks my fingers wet and clean.

§

Our brush pants soaked through
up to our thighs, snowmelt
soaking down into our boots where,
for the last hour, my feet have squished
in the puddles that I carry with me.

My pantcuffs and shoelaces frozen
solid around my ankles.

   Back at the truck, amid a big, cold
grassy prairie wind with the smell
of distance in it, my father and I set to
gutting the five pheasants we've shot.
I squint to the southwest, at the Loess
Hills, their draws shadowy and blue,
as if woodsmoke had settled in them—

   dunes created by windblown silt
during the retreat of the last glaciers,
much in the same manner as snowdrifts
massed along the lee side of line-
fences we have walked, strong
westerlies that lose momentum,
drop silty loads as they buffet
the eastern wall of an ancient
Missouri River valley.

   As we rinse the first gutted birds
in ice-cold water, the wind stings
our wet hands, and I stick mine into
warm entrails of the next bird,
letting them linger in this oddly
welcome heat.
                    §
For the Spanish bullfighter
it's the literal thing, but as for me
and my *querencia*, the place
where I feel safe, and serene,

where I know, while I am in it,
that no matter what happens
in life I will always be all right—
it's a ridge grown up in oak
and cedar, an abandoned
logging trail through northern
aspen and conifers, October
dawn, roseate chill, frost
feathering the fern duff, damp
of the autumn woods, its feast
of color, thunderous rise
and return of the messenger,
feathers loose and lovely
in the soft mouth of a bird dog.

§

The first day of the new year
loves an old meal, the slowest
food from another country,
where the last knowable part
of me started on a peasant
farm four centuries ago:
Hassenpfeffer
and its three day
song from the refrigerator,
a long, ancestral marinade.

§

The best days are always
the ones I walk into open
hearted without expectation,
the grouse neither as scarce
nor woodcock as thick
as the year before, each fall

bringing on an ache of joy
stronger than the last, many
seasons compressed in time
by my return to this single
place: a ring of birches
circling with outstretched
limbs, nature's version of
Picasso's *Dance of Youth*.

§

Long ago, before I immigrated
from the country of childhood,
I fell in love in with softer footfalls,
the cushion of the humus layer,
damp marrow of the woods
an hour before dawn. Now the creek
is only one long stride across
while the sugar maples are a full
story taller than I remember. Older,
all the unchanged flavors of earth
grow more delicious. It's time
rather than distance that separates
me from this other, this secret
sharer who carried nothing
but the lantern of his own eyes
across the creek and into the mist,
where now, like the son I still am,
I follow the father's pale glow further in.

Dream Songs for Autumn Prairies

Blackbirds

Disturbed by a dog
Bounding ahead of a man
The flock lifts from hidden
Roosts in ragged beige
Floodplain steppe
Spraying skyward
In startled chittering chaos

Until thousands of wings
Gather whirling as one
Sentient rhapsody
In flight like waves
Of music without sound
Improvisational notes
Of a single whole motion

Drawing together
Twisting and funneling
In extemporaneous pulses
Of shape-shifting complexity
Sinuous ink of a forgotten
Language evoking its own
Wordless magnificence

Clockworks

Rasp of cornstalks
Along fence-lines
Tattered husks
Torn, tormented
By incessant wind
Gusts that claw
The mind's dark
Soft tissues
My dead rustling
The parched rows
Calling out
With brittle
Incantations
From inside
A cornfield's
Unending maze
Without threshold
Entrance or exit
This ragged
Scroll of fields
Unfurling
To the circular
Rim of earth
Where faint
Mauve
Against
The horizon's
Cirrus
Of crop dust
Wind tower
Blades spin

Like wistful
Clockworks
Reversing
Time
In a distant
And lost country's
Mirage of dime
Store pin wheels
Grown immense
Since childhood

Pheasants

Field sparrows
Flick helplessly
From forked
Shrubs
Buffeted
Whipped away
By roiling
Gunmetal
Skies turning
Thick with sleet
To horizontal
Sting of ice pellets
Gusts of snow
Serpentine across
A cattail slough's
Black ice

Hiss of whiteout
Spinning its cocoon
Around the pilgrim
In orange vest
And stocking cap
His boyish
Face younger
Than memory
Finally summoned
By a car's
Futile honking

From the cattails
By way of a map

Of muskrat huts
His pointer's nose
Rubbed raw
By cutting reeds
Boot laces
Eyelashes
Shagged with ice

At the hospital
Dripping snowmelt
He smooths
The almond
Down
Etched with fine ovals
The soft
Iridescent copper
Plaited like a coat
Of feathered armor
Elegant tail spears
Brushed
With sure strokes
As of a calligrapher's
Rare black ink

He plucks one
Lays the quill
Across my
Newborn chest

Mountaineer

Via Facebook mutual friends reminded me
tomorrow's your birthday, the first
you won't be alive for.
Maybe I should post something
but what good would it do when
Nabil, my old friend's dead & gone,
just more cold meat in the ground.

I don't mind if others make themselves
feel better, we all want to feel better:
Let someone claim it was the new
epidemic that killed you, it's all the same
curse when you're addicted
to climb through a powder up your nose
higher and higher than the summit
of everyday life.

Everest's rarefied air, a grim
trail of rigor mortis.

Walking the Esker Road

I'm walking the path of the memory
    of a stream that flowed within a glacier,
        the esker road's narrow winding ridge
            through northern forest that drops
                away, steeply on both sides,
                forgetting

                  how I arrived here,
            or why, the reason for
        my present form, forgetting
      the shape of my body, the weight
    of my own face, my own name,
every name given to plants, trees,
shrubs, birds. Everything I
carried with me here

in becoming who I am,
heaviest to lightest burden, all insight,
    falling away as from a receding current,
        absorbed into the memory of water
            flowing through its tunnel of glacial
                ice, sand and gravel, stones, small

        boulders that still rise
      to the surface, after rains, or when
    frost heaves the thawing esker
road in exhalations that release
the last cool breaths

of a glacier. To walk
        in melodies cascading
                down from treetops along
                        the esker road is to forget
                                yourself, to assume
                                the identity of
                        a tamarack bog,
                the pungent, bosky mask
        of a fen, your companion
pausing to sniff fresh paw

prints and scat that bear
        a striking resemblance
                to her own, glints of
                        a beaver pond enjoying
                                its life as a pond, not
                        wishing to be anywhere
                or anything else.

Shannon and Anne

In my life the scales of time have
tipped toward the past, but does
that mean my future will be lighter?
I hope so. But then the weight
of time completely ignores justice,
an abundance of hale scot-free years for the
98-year-old Nazi war criminal as emaciated
Anne Frank with the immensity of her just-
blossoming genius doused by gas or typhus
at Bergen-Belsen—not unlike my daughter's
hockey teammate Shannon who died
after withering in the daily concentration
camp of a cancer ward: *My life is going*
to mean something to someone, somewhere
she wrote in her journals. Meanwhile, merciless
time bestows its ceaseless river of days
that so far keep on coming, a strong
current of mercy which Shannon still rides
into the future on the gift of her brain
tissue that might someday, somewhere
give another young girl more time, perhaps
grace of a long full life reaching far beyond
her own nascent bloom. Such singular
waiting-to-be-discovered wildflowers
that take root in courage only to be stifled
while their first nonpareil radiance lives on.

for Shannon O'Hara

Song and Dance Man

Vast indifference of the universe
stretches out in every direction,
relentlessly marching you along
its galactic path toward non-being—
yet it can't touch your life
from the trail you're walking,
where you pause to witness
the spherical dance of your feet,
your tethered body whirling,
bare feet plunged in new
tufts of spring, clover cold
with morning dew; *shinrin-
yoku* through sun-shot pastels
of birch and aspen, essence
of cedar and fern, wild plum
thickets in full blossom, glacial
breath of the river exhaling mist,
woodpeckers' incantatory tremolos,
irresistible bowstring of the south
wind's tree-rubbing-tree music,
creak and sway of the forest's
old, warped floor in motion
with greening earth herself.

Capturing the Moment

1.

Sudden drabness of that lone heirloom
apple tree across emerald swales of new
meadow grass startled—like news
of someone's unexpected
death. Yesterday when I forgot
my camera this tree was in full
glorious spring bloom, like my daughter
and her friends—young, animated,
magnificent in dresses and tuxes—I photographed
that same afternoon before they headed
off to prom. Now the glowing almost lunar
soft profusion of pink and white
blossoms had suddenly dropped with a mute
despondency squalling through
my heart like a sun shower. While beside

2.

the Root River, cumbersome Nikon slung
heavily around my neck, I stared into the very
heart of the moment, a rapids
in ceaseless flow, the ever-fleeting
ever-fleeing moment always flowing
into itself, current ever moving on yet
forever renewing itself, the moment always
freeing its present moment. As kids, we captured

3.

hordes of furry bumblebees from wild bergamot
between a metal lid clapped over the lip

of a mayonnaise jar—an imprisoned
frenzy of moments that slowly
suffocated. Such relentless pursuit—butterflies
we caught with nets lighting on milkweed
in moist native (mesic) prairie that survived
in a narrow strip along the railroad
embankment—careful not to mar the delicate
powder and pattern of their wings as we slid
a pin through the beefy shiver
of thorax into corkboard, our otherworldly
collections of stilled
wings spread in swirls and hues—
swallowtail, monarch, morning
cloak, sulphur, satyr, buckeye, viceroy, question mark,
admiral, frittilary, checkerspot, bluet—now all
crumbled to dust, far too late to set
the moment free again.

for Jerry Olson

Staving Off Despair

I rejoice in Oshie—canine coat
autumn-beige with fox-red accents—
poised as if in meditation, beginner's
mind of paw cocked on point, foreleg
softly curled at the knuckle, supple
and low-slung, deeply composed
yet sleek with intensity, divining rod
of nose twitching as if over some
secret vein of ore, or life-giving
fount of artesian groundwater; eyes
locked on an inert dirt-worn tennis
ball that squeaks manically, shrill
in the clutch of her muzzle: such
tantalizing repetition, glorious
routine, hours of fetch, retrieving
over and over, every time a thrill
as if for the first time, trotting
back beaming with an accomplished
jubilant fellow-creature smile. I hurl it
far as I can; relish her mad insistent dash,
an earth-thumping sprint into ferns
riffling with unfettered pursuit, fur
between her pads like my knees
as a child stained by summer grass.

Handsaw

Hard to throw away the old handsaw
even as half its ash handle disintegrates
mid-stroke through a storm-
toppled maple limb, blade dull
as old bovine teeth chewing cud,
insolent with rust—red as kelp—
left out in summer rains and buried
all one winter—worn by the years
of hand-sawing through sheath
green skins of living branches, crib
and dog-house projects, a swing-set's
dense green-treated, surging with preserving
juices, like at the beginning of a long
marriage, dark and new. Even gripping
half its greyed handle, as if sea-weathered
through some ship's fatal voyage, it's a tarnished
mirror I want to hang onto, one side reflecting
the other, heartwood-entrenched work,
heat-friction and scars ingrained in steel,
and nothing imaginary, except with miserable
dimness, the two figures who gradually
withdrew from each other's wildest ideals,
as together they sawed their way down,
never giving up, though sometimes wanting
or threatening to do so amid the difficult
toil and sweat, all they could do to keep
up the effort, as if sawing into a stump
much too massive, one they refused
to believe that overmatched blade
might never make it through.

Garden Time

Damp earth again stains your hands and knees
as you kneel with a trowel, digging a root clump,
gently patting the earth as you transplant an iris,
moving certain perennials while thinning others.
How content and focused you are chiseling
wild mint that's flourished and spread
overtaking too much of the strawberry patch
our kids once searched with stubby fingers,
delighted to discover its ripe prone berries
hiding under low dense leaf clusters,
young faces rapt as a monarch or yellow
swallowtail fluttered the swamp milkweed
that sprang up mysteriously one summer,
somehow seeded of its own accord.
The taciturn hollyhocks you nurtured
into bloom climbing their trellis slowly,
season after season, as if keeping pace
with the thin gray streak sprouted from the roots
in the part of your otherwise auburn hair,
my head now bald as baby wrens chittering
from the birdhouse their mother burrows into
with a tiny grub clenched between her beak.

Fireflies

All those bright perennial years we shared
in our marriage house tending its gardens,
neighbor kids dashing through a sprinkler
as if from a fountain of days
that would never run out.
And still, I can't remember even one
summer night we opened every window
to let the cool breeze drift in,
a few last pale bird cries,
maybe the serenade of crickets,
our dog flopped with disinterest,
asleep, her fur soft against our shins.
After our exhausted forms parted
in the darkness one or the other might have
risen just before the abyss
to bring back a glass of ice water;
footsteps creaking the wooden staircase,
the dog trailing with a comforting staccato
click of its nails against the oak floor.
Maybe while you were in the kitchen,
a silhouette filling a glass at the sink,
you might have peered out the window
briefly at a night just like this one—
hundreds of fireflies flashing back,
like glimpses from our future
drifting the garden ferns till dawn.

County Fair

For a single week in high summer our drab
town turns festive with Midway neon,
carnies barking wild-eyed challenges
luring teens toward calliope booths,
the air rifle range, flashing lights
of the Ferris wheel spinning at dusk
night air sultry with sizzling grease,
funnel cakes, cheese curds, pronto pups.
I like to stay late, studying tattoos,
a divine feminine angel, fairies, bird
and animal totems, roses, butterflies
of the psyche, a pair of praying hands,
a snake devouring its own tail,
admiring all the wild manifestations
people feel so strongly about
they are willing to let someone ingrain
with permanent ink onto their bodies.

Even more, I like to go back
just before dawn, stroll the livestock barns
amid the repose of sunburned
farm kids asleep on cots, camped out
in the sawdust among their cows,
lambs and horses, finding
that which most eludes me,
my soul medicine in the quiet
as I slowly wander the aisles, stall
to stall beneath the coo and choke
of pigeons huddled in the rafters,
among the bleating lambs, swishing

tails and soft nickers, studying my own
manifestations in the grainy light,
waiting for an inner lyric that might yet
gift itself from the eyes of an animal,
the rise of an image that breathes
like someone for whom I would lay
my life down in the straw.

Magnetic Rock

My eyes still carry
A boreal pine-scented light
From that invincible summer
I worked at a canoe outfitter
In the far north bristling
With youth and a voyageur's *joie de vivre*

I mostly scrubbed blackened pots & pans
Scorched by campfire

On one of my rare days off I hiked
Up a rugged, boulder-strewn trail
To an ancient rock monolith
The spire of a glacial erratic full of ore
A magnetic rock with an aura
That drove my compass wild
Its frenzied needle whirling
Faster and faster

How could I ever forget
Jill with her bare feet swishing
Gunflint Lake's dark lilt
Waiting for me in a white blouse
By starlight at the end of the dock

Money

Days I worry too much about money
My anxiety drives me indoors
Toiling to provide for three children
Far from the river where I long to be
Other times even as my debts
Mount I can't stand the notion
I'm pissing away my life on nonsense
Beyond the barest essentials
A crust of bread in my pocket,
I grow carefree, smiling back
As the laughing river flows by
Giving away its currency in rise
Forms, wild brown trout sipping
The mayfly hatch all around
My burden light—lighter
Than casting a weightless fly

for Greg Brown

Milky Way

Bleary-eyed and up too late
Well beyond midnight
Scribbling in my notebook
The poem I'm trying to write
Gets distracted and lurches up
For another big glass of wine
But why should I care?
Out the kitchen window
Night's straining
Her waist so I can peer
Through the chiffon
Lace of the Milky Way

Cranes

Twilight on Easter morning I was excited
To show my 19-year-old daughter
A pair of mating sandhill cranes
Shale feathers soft as woodsmoke
Scarlet head patches like embers
As they leapt their courtship dance
Through a mist of vernal snowmelt
By the time we quickly drove back there
Like her whole childhood the cranes
Had drifted away into the willows

Spring Mushrooms

In my headstrong know-it-all youth I railed
Against development and suburban sprawl
This land is your land, this land is my land
Wide open spaces for all, sea to shining sea
My young wife and I settled into each other
Like an old stucco we bought in the city core
Where I relished the near-constant repairs
Quarter-sawn red oak hardwood floors
Craftsmanship of built-in oak bookcases
Cobwebs in the dank unfinished basement
Old boiler and asbestos-wrapped pipes
Clank and ping of the radiators
Useless cistern a racoon once fell in
And tried to claw its way back up the walls
Acrobatics of bats living in our attic
Fluttering the yard at dusk
In January a quarter century later high on a ladder
Chipping away ice dams I finally agree to move
Now I like our new house at the far edge of town
And hardly mind at all all the new rooftops
Popping up everywhere like spring mushrooms
Everything we build a kind of fallible toadstool
Destined to crumble and rot back into itself
Meanwhile I wander the forest out my back door
In search of morels with a Spore Boy mesh bag
When I find a small flourish I shake each one well
In order to make certain I sprinkle a lot of spore

Gravel Pit

My oldest son's a well-trained killer
Meant to be lethal if the time comes
Once a tot playing with green plastic
Toy army guys, our backyard
Sandbox has grown and morphed
Into a make-believe theatre of war
The broad abandoned gravel pit
Gouged from an esker at the cabin
Where he and his college military
Pals wearing night-vision goggles
Stalk then rush mock-human targets
Unleashing rounds with AR-15s
While from real deer stands
Inside the heart of my heart of darkness
In the surrounding forest I imagine
Enemy snipers taking fatal aim

Hunting the Sun

Hiking the autumn forest with my father
Breathless shouldering both our heavy packs
Through a tonic of rich and deepening color
The labor of sustaining our love somehow
Grows lighter with the swiftness of time
He moves more slowly than I remember
Yet I am content to let him take the lead
Study his shadow in motion over the earth
While kettles of migrating broad-winged
Hawks soar on afternoon thermals
Thousands streaming south above the ridge
Hunting the warmth of the sun

Splitting Rounds

In our time people seem to want everyday
Life easier & more comfortable with least
Resistance automated by the latest gadgets
Fingertips constantly tapping devices
That spin tangled webs of information
Confused, I don't know what to do
I head for my wood chopping block
Splitting rounds with axe and wedge
Happily drenched, my palms blistered

Last Round-Up

In April 1997 as the Hale-Bopp Comet flared
Its swift luminous mane across a night sky
Naturally, I imagined it might be Jesus
Bareback on a magnificent cosmic horse
Loping through a nearby meadow of the universe
This rugged 33-year-old Palestinian
Divine cowboy forever in the prime of life
Yodeling on down the trail deciding it wasn't
Quite time for this planet's last big round-up

Arctic Dust

I don't know how I become this suicidal
As if generations of coal miner's dust
Settled at birth into the *aveoli* of my soul
On the winter solstice 24 hours of pure
Darkness still leaks from Earth's fontanel
Which is why in summer I make my eyes
And skin drink, in huge greedy gulps, like lemonade,
The blinding light of the sun, to last these months
When that dust, now frozen, snows from the arctic

Evening Cumulous

Once a hale athletic youth
A certain age just beyond the mirror
Of adolescence gazing
Into the rising swell of his biceps
Forearms corded and rippling
Blue veins like raised creek deltas
Torso as if sculpted by chisels
Of a powerful river cascading
Down the gorge of his body
Molding it in the image
Of giant river boulders
Atop which female hikers
Pause to sit and ponder
Stacks of evening cumulous
Massed on the horizon
Like a mountain range
Beyond which rise higher
Ever more magnificent
Peaks he sets out to climb
By Sisyphean force of will
Higher and farther
Convinced he'll find
One day no matter
How arduous the journey
That timeless
Tibetan Lamasery
Shangri La

Dead Bird Dog

My first dog Rose stares into me daily with dark-lit
Acorn eyes & white muzzle from a framed portrait
As if I could still touch her moist divining nose
Stroke the velvet semaphores of her fox-red ears
More time walking side-by-side over many seasons
Than with my wife and our three grown children
How will I ever finish mourning my eager companion
Who, carefully crumbing her grave, I buried along
With last of my youth wrapped in worn hunting shirts
In unbroken prairie sod beneath a sentinel burr oak

Dog Spirit

Weary of every pursuit, poetry and life stale
What helps most is to take a drive with Oshie
A yellow Labrador who rides on her haunches
Muzzle twitching out the passenger window
Seining the wind's secret trove of scents
Supple velvet ears flopping aloft as she kisses
Joy in the moment without consideration
My canine companion in love with the world
Peering out as if every common bird in flight
Opens an immense world of delight

Shrine by the Lake

It wasn't easy building this pleasure
Dome sauna sweat lodge shrine of private religion
Felling four tall red pines with an axe
Dragging each heavy log by cant hook and rope
Peeling bark with bark spud and draw knife
The constant *chuck chuck chuck* of an adze
Through a summer welter of deer flies
Chewing tiny bleeding divots from my flesh
Yet my hands found relief chinking the logs
Within a cool viscous mixture of clay, silt & ash
My mind, meditation in mortaring round glacial
Esker stones that rose with painstaking
Slowness from cairn to hearth
To spire of finished chimney

First ceremonial woodsmoke now rising
As birch and spruce pass into flame
Forest transfigures into fire
Blazing in an old lumberjack camp barrel stove
Fresh-cut cedar sprigs sweating
Redolent on a basket of sauna rocks
Selected from shoreline shallows
Squash and egg-shaped stones
That traveled a continent by glacier
To shape the shoreline of Courtney Lake
Offspring of a buried block of slowly melting ice
Lake water that still freezes over
In image of the ice that gave it birth

Time in this shrine by the lake
As a voyage of fire and ice
Of rock that started as fire
And water that began as ice
That unites rock with water
Igneous magma flow with glacial ice
Heat and steam that rises as spirit
Flowing back into the body
Marrow of the hearth
With the man breathing it in

for Denny Scherer

The Edge

Now a raging alcoholic, my old friend's
Part time job is sending me inane texts
Mostly U-Tube clips of David Letterman
Interviews 30+ years after our shared youth
When he brilliantly edited the junk I wrote
For our high school paper *Inside the Aquarium*
J.R. was once a journalist of immense talent
Yet could never write as well without an edge
That grew to a chasm of vodka he crossed
From one unforgiving deadline to the next
Now he can't write at all, sober or drunk
In fear that if he even tries to write while
Sober he'll need to get too drunk to write

Autumn Snow Squall

He wakes to the light of himself
Sober in a bright new morning
All superfluous work left behind
Cell phone turned off to distractions
No news from the outside world
Ready pen in eager hand
Coffee and notebook on the table
Chickadees and nuthatches
Flitting at the tube feeders
Greedy for black-oil sunflower seed
Five young maples vermilion
As last night's campfire flames
In view across the old field
Meadow brooding with low clouds
Darker now as a snow squall whips
Its aster and goldenrod grasses
A whole field into motion
Flurries sprinting thick
With the dust of ghost horses
Galloping their spirit world
Flurries that whir then cease
And settle on everything soft
As a plague of summer moths

While Oshie the dog naps
Her head's soft impression
Upon a pillow on the futon
A kettle of cold rainwater
Drawn from the rain barrel

Wheezing on the stovetop
Sooty remnant storm clouds whisk by
A murder of crows flap and sail
Slick and shining across the field

Outside he pours steaming rain
Water in cascades over his head
Shivering as he soaps and washes
Stinging cold interstices between
Hot rinsing pours of rainwater
Naked in an icy wind
That swirls the grove of spindled
Old-growth Bigtooth Aspen
Tall and straight as matchsticks
Each fresh gust striking their bushy tops
As if his body might burst into flame

Milton Gerard

Lofted on snowshoes
As if the compression of my steps,
Hallowed marks in the shape
Of beavertail, as if the spirit
Of this prime furbearer
Trailing me across fresh snow,
Might help move winter forward
As I set out in lilac moonlight
Spliced with long tree shadows
Setting tracks before sunrise's
Faint lime and pink bands
My wandering loops and spurs
Creating a kind of personal
Milton Gerard signature
Through the hardwoods
Checking my traplines
Along trout stream banks
Through thick river bottoms
Via a map of muskrat huts
In desolate sloughs
As if each hike among many
Somehow gives me a sense
Of companionship following
Fresh fellow creature tracks
My only respite from loneliness
Because I live by killing
With remorse everything I love
As if my own survival
Or salvation's a faint

Arctic whisper
Always in my ear
Soft honeycombed collapse
And upward sift
Through wicker sinew
A taut latticework
Bound to curved ash frames
Hung like dreamcatchers
At eventide on nails
Against knotty pine
Their fresh coats of ship
Varnish glistening in firelight
My sleep an amber hum
Insulated by deep drifts

for Tony Gerard

Algific Talus Slope

On a north-facing rim of limestone
Bluff also known as a *Maderate Cliff*
In a valley cut by the Great Flood
The sound of wind from an earlier
Cooler epoch swirls the stately tops
Of a remnant pocket of white pines
Fluttering the leaves of attendant
Paper birch and mountain maple
While below in an occluded glen
Along a slope of fractured limestone
Fed cold air by subterranean ice caves
Boreal disjuncts:
Canada Yew
Balsam Fir,
Dwarf Alder
Red-berried Elder
Rare Leedy's Roseroot (found
Only here on earth)
Cling to ledges and crevices
Further down liverwort and mosses
Drape the dark seeping rockface
Amid a cascade of arctic ferns
That shiver in cool luxuriance
Oxymoronic in the humid July breeze
Descended from Pleistocene man
I declare kinship with Ice Age relicts
Pleistocene land snails and arctic ferns
Basking in shared postglacial pleasure
In summer exhalations of ice-cooled
Breath from a vent in steep karst cliff

Live Water

My closest friend and I grow older
Old since we met in kindergarten
A fraught river of days carrying us
Tumultuous with love and death
Early death of his father
Early death of his brother
Onerous with responsibilities
Marriage and raising children
Months and years downstream
From our once-frequent visits
My hair's all fallen out
He still has a thick mane
My stubble greys and his chin sags
But we don't worry as the inexorable
Current of days sweeps us far
Out of sight from one another
Our friendship's like live water
That can't help itself
But to keep on flowing
As from a spring upstream
From which time never runs out
Running water that's always there
Even when we are not
As if there is no time between us
Today when we finally embrace
As if I'd never left his presence
Like the sound of the stream
As we hike down to fish
Rising into us through the trees
for Lane Underdahl

Evening Sketch along a Trout Stream

Silhouette of cattle
Grazing at peace
On the brow of a green hill

Their massed forms
Shuffling slowly
With swishing tails
Huffing breaths

When one begins
To bellow a nameless
Complaint against life
Over and over

At which I stop casting
Pull myself up the bank
And prop my fly-rod

Against a limestone outcrop
As if there might be
Something more I can do

For this cow bawling
Its tireless plight
Other than listen

Until its unbated suffering
Finally fades with the herd
Into the fold of a distant hill

Enchanted by the familiar
Trill of evening crickets
I take out my notebook
To write about the acrobatic
Flutter and feint of brown
Bats in flight over the stream

The glints of trout leaping
As caddisflies flutter
And skitter across its surface

Straining for a poem
When I shiver at what I
Didn't notice beside me
On a rock shelf

There all the while
Shedding its skin
In a translucent coil

Peeling away
As it pours itself
Over a ledge

Then slides
Through concealing
Grass

for Justin Watkins

Last Night

I scrambled for newspaper and kindling,
broke free and split huge iced-over logs;
sweated, wheelbarrowing uphill through
snowpack more strain than my legs
wanted to bear; finally struck matches
with numb trembling fingers, tips
half frozen, chest heaving for breath,
my lungs a bellows blasting smoke
into flame, on short notice,
for my daughter and her friends.

Empty Adirondack chairs tipped over,
toppled like sculpture in boot-pocked
snow the morning after a bonfire,
around its limestone fire-ring, cryptic
as Stonehenge. Last night's altar
ablaze, sparks shooting star-
ward with feverish abandon,
all the short-lived ardor of youth,
its heat still smoldering. No celebrants
left this morning except me staring out
at this strange, beautifully ordained
arrangement of empty chairs. Last
night's solstice tribe chanting
ancient hymns, tender ones about the birth
of a son, belting out old fashioned
festive carols, while passing a bottle
of Fireball, their communal cup,
amid blooms of spontaneous laughter,
firefly glow and flicker of iPhone

screens, Snapchat and text messages,
fingertips frenzied as summer bees.

Later, they danced their generation's
ritual throb of hip-hop around the bonfire
hurtling at its peak, a pagan
band of college kids arrived home
reveling in the rebirth of the sun,
forces of nature that drive the green
fuse, while I stood far back, in delights
and shadows, among our lighted pines
twinkling triumph over the yard's
darkness and dormant earth.

Sound of a Trout Stream through Trees

When my life is over;
when fly-rods I loved to cast,
beloved shotguns handed down
or auctioned off; when all
the trees I planted are taller
than my life was long;
that is, when I'm suddenly
dead forever; when great
grandkids have, perhaps,
only the dimmest
recollection of a resigned
wizened face; after all five
thousand books I read
are sold, dumped, or divvied
among my heirs; after
the sound of a trout stream
through trees; after my ashes
scatter and I'm only a few
stray molecules absorbed
into the Mississippi's sluggish
Gulfward flow; when I am
no one's memory; weathered
name on stone; when that
time comes; after I've
lived off the few songs
that breached the threshold
of my tongue, and died
by everything I held in.

Acknowledgements

The author, me, wishes to express my heartfelt appreciation to the editors of the following publications, in which some of these poems, often in earlier versions, first appeared:

The Café Review
Cave Wall
Crossings at Carnegie Poet Artist Collaboration
Goodreads Monthly Poetry Contest
Great River Review
The Green Blade
Iddie
Interpoezia
Lost Lake Folk Opera
Main Channel Voices
Rochester Post Bulletin
Rural America Writer's Center Tribute Book to Dean & Sally Harrington
Verse Wisconsin

I also wish to gratefully acknowledge all the friends, colleagues, teachers, professors, editors, fellow writers, and family members who have helped make a part-time writing life possible for me.

In no particular order, I want to thank these closest friends for the grace, patience, and insight they have showed and given me—without them and their belief in me, this first book would never have come to fruition: To Lane Underdahl, who always believed in me, even when I no longer believed in myself. Your lifelong companionship and wisdom have made an essential, existential difference in my life; to Steve Melander, for starting our text thread, and for your lively mind, loyalty, and abiding friendship; to G.R. Anderson, Jr., eternal gratitude, for all the lively conversations we had over the last several years about writing, literature, art, journalism, and music; and to Nabil Daniel Streets, easily the most intuitive person I ever knew, once as close as brothers, may he rest in peace.

To John Olson, multitalented man who keeps the spirit of Hunter alive, yet somehow still manages to watch over me; for friendship that grows as much at it endures—we are always with each other in Rockland!

To Delores (Dee) Nelson and Melodee Margaret Monicken, extraordinary Orono High School English teachers who initiated and facilitated my fall into love with language and literature. To my undergraduate college professors, both living and dead—Wayne Carver, Seymour (Sy) Schuster, George Soule, Keith Harrison, Constance Walker, Walter Benjamin, and poet Greg Hewett—thank you for your ardent devotion to the teaching of literature, your passion for the great works, and for putting up with my incessant questions. To my graduate school advisors, mentors, and workshop leaders at the Vermont College of Fine Arts (VCFA)—Roger Weingarten, Leslie Ullman, Mary Ruefle, Betsy Sholl, David Wojahn, David Jauss, William Olsen, and Nancy Eimers—for showing me the way through the example of your work, for the kindness of your toughest criticism, and for your insights into your individual approaches to the demands of writing. Also, to Joseph Millar, whose poetry I love, along with the late Marvin Bell and Madeline DeFrees, whose triumvirate of lectures the lone semester I attended the Pacific MFA program had a profound impact. And to my fellow graduate students at VCFA for their generosity in helping me strive to make my work as good as this maker could make it—especially Jennifer Elise Foerster, a poet whose work I deeply admire, from afar.

Heartfelt thanks and more than nine bows of gratitude to my publisher, Tom Driscoll, Managing editor at Shipwreckt Books and the Up On Big Rock Poetry Series, for his patience, kindness, wit, wisdom, and enthusiasm for my work. Emilio DeGrazia for your inscription—that my time would one day come. Justin Watkins, kindred spirit, for your generous text and email exchanges about poetry and books—for writing about subjects antithetical to our times—and for inspiring me through your *sui generis* work.

Lastly, I want to thank my family, especially my wife's grandfather, Ed Sharkey, an Irishman who created the Mary Lake Library, whose love of literature and the natural world remains deeply influential and inspiring; my parents and my in-laws for their abiding love, support, and guidance; my three children for their deep interest in books and ideas; my son Sam for the breadth and depth he brings to our always lively and interesting conversations about life, history, movies, and literature—and for inspiring me through his gifts for music and lyrical songwriting; my daughter Sophie for always challenging me to wake up every morning striving to be a better human being than I was the day before, and for our shared love and appreciation of the outdoor life and natural world; my son Liam for his keen emotional intelligence, wellspring of love for people, and untrammeled enthusiasm for life—without whom I might never have come to peace with middle age; my daughter-in-law Sarah for setting the bar high by her example of always setting the bar higher for herself. You each make me immensely proud to be your dad.

To my wife, best friend, confidante, critic, advisor, psychologist, counselor, companion, life partner, and soulmate, Ellen. Who has shown me that the greatest love of all is one that endures. This book is for her.

About the Author

Dan Butterfass lives in Rochester, Minnesota with his family and divides his time between the Med City and a cabin in the Big Woods of the Driftless Area in southeastern Minnesota. Butterfass holds an MFA from the Vermont College of Fine Arts, and has made his living, among other ways, as a college English instructor, outdoor writer, bookshop proprietor, and entrepreneur in the field of tourism.

www.ingramcontent.com/pod-product-compliance
Lightning Source LLC
Chambersburg PA
CBHW080606270326

41928CB00016B/2952